NOTHING TO HIDE

Nothing
to
Hide

The False Tradeoff
between Privacy
and Security

Daniel J. Solove

Yale

UNIVERSITY PRESS
New Haven & London

To Pamela and Griffin, with love

Copyright © 2011 by Daniel J. Solove.

All rights reserved.

This book may not be reproduced, in whole or in part, including illustrations, in any form (beyond that copying permitted by Sections 107 and 108 of the U.S. Copyright Law and except by reviewers for the public press), without written permission from the publishers.

Yale University Press books may be purchased in quantity for educational, business, or promotional use. For information, please e-mail sales.press@yale.edu (U.S. office) or sales@yaleup.co.uk (U.K. office).

Set in Electra type by Integrated Publishing Solutions.
Printed in the United States of America.

The Library of Congress has cataloged the hardcover edition as follows:

Solove, Daniel J., 1972–
    Nothing to hide : the false tradeoff between privacy and security / Daniel J. Solove.
        p. cm.
    Includes bibliographical references and index.
    ISBN 978-0-300-17231-7 (cloth : alk. paper)   1. Privacy, Right of—United
States.   2. Law enforcement—United States   3. National security—Law and
legislation—United States   I. Title.
    KF1262.S65 2011
    342.7308′58—dc22   2010049542

ISBN 978-0-300-17233-1 (pbk.)

A catalogue record for this book is available from the British Library.

Contents

Contents

Preface

The idea for this book began with an essay I wrote a few years ago called *"I've Got Nothing to Hide" and Other Misunderstandings of Privacy*. After I posted it online, I was stunned by the attention it received across the Internet and in the media. I realized that there was a lot of interest in the debate between privacy and national security and that the same group of arguments came up again and again. I also realized that there were many misimpressions about the law.

Increasingly, I've found it frustrating when I hear certain arguments in favor of heightened security that have become quite prevalent. I believe they have skewed the balance between privacy and security too much to the security side. One of my goals in this book is to respond to some of these arguments.

I have written this book for a general audience, avoiding legal jargon and wonky policy analysis. I've presented more detailed policy proposals in my law review articles, but for this book, I focus on the general arguments and principles rather than technical minutiae. Of course, the details are important, but even more important are the basic concepts and themes of the debate. I hope that this book will put to rest certain arguments so that the debate can move ahead in more fruitful ways.

Although I have focused primarily on American law, the arguments and ideas in the debate are universal. Despite a few differences, the law in many countries operates similarly to American law, and it often uses the same techniques to regulate government information gathering. The arguments and policy recommendations I propose in this book are meant to be relevant not just in the United States but also in other nations whose lawmakers are struggling with these important issues.

Some of the material for this book was adapted from a few of my law review articles. These articles are much more extensive than their adaptations in this book, and they are often very different in form and argument. I have not fully incorporated these articles here, so they remain independent works. I recommend that you check them out if you want a more technical treatment of some of the issues in this book: *Fourth Amendment Pragmatism*, 51 BOSTON COLLEGE LAW REVIEW (forthcoming); *Data Mining and the Security-Liberty Debate*, 74 UNIVERSITY OF CHICAGO LAW REVIEW 343 (2008); *"I've Got Nothing to Hide" and Other Misunderstandings of Privacy*, 44 SAN DIEGO LAW REVIEW 745 (2007); *The First Amendment as Criminal Procedure*, 84 NEW YORK UNIVERSITY LAW REVIEW 112 (2007); *Fourth Amendment Codification and Professor Kerr's Misguided Call for Judicial Deference*, 74 FORDHAM LAW REVIEW 747 (2005); *Melville's Billy Budd and Security in Times of Crisis*, 26 CARDOZO LAW REVIEW 2443 (2005); *Reconstructing Electronic Surveillance Law*, 72 GEORGE WASHINGTON LAW REVIEW 1264 (2004). My thinking has evolved since the publication of many of these articles, so this book represents my most current view of the issues. Moreover, writing this book forced me to think more broadly about the topic of privacy versus security, and there are many issues I address here that I haven't addressed before.

Many people helped me greatly with this project. My wife, Pamela, provided constant support and encouragement as well as superb suggestions on the manuscript. Many others have made immensely helpful comments on this book: Danielle Citron, Tommy

Crocker, Deven Desai, Chris Hoofnagle, Orin Kerr, Raymond Ku, Paul Ohm, Neil Richards, and Michael Sullivan. I would also like to thank my research assistant, Matthew Albanese, for his help. My editor, Michael O'Malley, was a joy to work with, and my copyeditor, Dan Heaton, carefully reviewed the manuscript. My agent, Susan Schulman, provided excellent guidance and encouragement throughout the publication process.

Introduction

"We must be willing to give up some privacy if it makes
us more secure."

"If you've got nothing to hide, you shouldn't worry about
government surveillance."

"We shouldn't second-guess security officials."

"In national emergencies, rights must be cut back,
but they'll be restored later on."

We hear these arguments all the time. We hear them in the
conversations we have each day with our family, friends,
and colleagues. We hear them in the media, which is buzz-
ing with stories about government information gathering, such as the
Total Information Awareness program, the airline passenger screening program, and the surveillance of people's phone calls conducted
by the secretive National Security Agency. We hear them made by
politicians and security officials. And we hear them made by judges
deciding how to balance security measures with people's constitutional rights.

These arguments are part of the debate between privacy and
security. The consequences of the debate are enormous, for both privacy and security are essential interests, and the balance we strike
between them affects the very foundations of our freedom and democracy. In contemporary times—especially after the terrorist attacks
on September 11, 2001—the balance has shifted toward the security

side of the scale. The government has been gathering more information about people and engaging in more surveillance. Technology is giving the government unprecedented tools for watching people and amassing information about them—video surveillance, location tracking, data mining, wiretapping, bugging, thermal sensors, spy satellites, X-ray devices, and more. It's nearly impossible to live today without generating thousands of records about what we watch, read, buy, and do—and the government has easy access to them.

The privacy-security debate profoundly influences how these government activities are regulated. But there's a major problem with the debate: Privacy often loses out to security when it shouldn't. Security interests are readily understood, for life and limb are at stake, while privacy rights remain more abstract and vague. Many people believe they must trade privacy in order to be more secure. And those on the security side of the debate are making powerful arguments to encourage people to accept this tradeoff.

These arguments, however, are based on mistaken views about what it means to protect privacy and the costs and benefits of doing so. The debate between privacy and security has been framed incorrectly, with the tradeoff between these values understood as an all-or-nothing proposition. But protecting privacy need not be fatal to security measures; it merely demands oversight and regulation. We can't progress in the debate between privacy and security because the debate itself is flawed.

The law suffers from related problems. It seeks to balance privacy and security, but systematic problems plague the way the balancing takes place. When evaluating security measures, judges are often too deferential to security officials. And the law gets caught up in cumbersome tests to determine whether government information gathering should be subjected to oversight and regulation, resulting in uneven and incoherent protection. The law sometimes stringently protects against minor privacy invasions yet utterly fails to protect against major ones. For example, the Fourth Amendment will protect you when a police officer squeezes the outside of your duffel bag—yet it won't stop the government from obtaining all your Google search queries or your credit card records.

The privacy-security debate and the law have a two-way relationship. Many arguments in the debate are based on false assumptions about how the law protects privacy. And the law has been shaped by many flawed arguments in the debate, which have influenced legislation and judicial opinions.

I propose to demonstrate how privacy interests can be better understood and how security interests can be more meaningfully evaluated. I aim to refute the recurrent arguments that skew the privacy-security debate toward the security side. I endeavor to show how the law frequently fixes on the wrong questions, such as *whether* privacy should be protected rather than *how* it should be protected. Privacy often can be protected without undue cost to security. In instances when adequate compromises can't be achieved, the tradeoff can be made in a manner that is fair to both sides. We can reach a better balance between privacy and security. We must. There is too much at stake to fail.

A Short History of Privacy and Security

The law and policy addressing privacy and security is quite extensive, involving the U.S. Constitution, federal statutes, state constitutions, and state statutes. Quite a number of federal agencies are involved, such as the Federal Bureau of Investigation (FBI), Central Intelligence Agency (CIA), National Security Agency (NSA), Department of Homeland Security (DHS), Transportation Security Administration (TSA), and others. There are countless state and local police departments. In order to understand how privacy and security are balanced, I will first explain briefly how we got to where we are today.

The Right to Privacy

People have cared about privacy since antiquity. The Code of Hammurabi protected the home against intrusion, as did ancient Roman law.[1] The early Hebrews had laws safeguarding against surveillance. And in England, the oft-declared principle that the home is one's "castle" dates to the late fifteenth century.[2] Eavesdropping was long protected against in the English common law, and in 1769, the legal scholar William Blackstone defined it as listening "under walls or windows, or the eaves of a house, to hearken after discourse, and thereupon to frame slanderous and mischievous tales."[3]

The right to privacy emerged in countries all around the world in many different dimensions. Protections arose against invasions of privacy by nosy neighbors and gossipy newspapers, as well as against government searches and seizures. In England, for example, the idea that citizens should be free from certain kinds of intrusive government searches developed during the early 1500s.[4]

In America, at the time of the Revolutionary War, a central privacy issue was freedom from government intrusion. The Founders detested the use of general warrants to conduct sweeping searches of people's homes and to seize their papers and writings.[5] As Patrick Henry declared: "They may, unless the general government be restrained by a bill of rights, or some similar restrictions, go into your cellars and rooms, and search, ransack, and measure, everything you eat, drink, and wear. They ought to be restrained within proper bounds."[6]

These sentiments were enshrined into the Bill of Rights. The Fourth Amendment to the U.S. Constitution prevents the government from conducting "unreasonable searches and seizures." Government officials must obtain judicial approval before conducting a search through a warrant that is supported by probable cause. The Fifth Amendment affords individuals a privilege against being compelled to incriminate themselves.

The Rise of Police Systems and the FBI

Security is also a universal value, tracing back to antiquity. People have long looked to their governments to keep them secure from bandits, looters, and foreign invaders. They have also wanted to ensure social order by protecting against robberies, rapes, murders, and other crimes. But for a long time, many countries lacked police forces. In medieval England, for example, posses hunted down criminals and summarily executed them. Later on, patrolling amateurs protected communities, but they rarely investigated crimes.[7]

By the twentieth century, police forces had transformed into organized units of professionals.[8] In the United States, policing developed locally at the city and state levels, not nationwide. The rise of the mafia and organized crime required law enforcement to find means to learn about what crimes these groups were planning. The government began to increase prosecution of certain consensual crimes, such as gambling, the use of alcohol during Prohibition, and the trafficking of drugs. Unlike robberies or assaults, which are often reported to the police, these crimes occurred through transactions in an underground market. Undercover agents and surveillance became key tools for detecting these crimes.

The FBI emerged in the early years of the twentieth century, the brainchild of Attorney General Charles Bonaparte. He twice asked Congress to authorize the creation of a detective force in the Department of Justice (DOJ), but he was rebuffed both times.[9] Congress worried about secret police prying into the privacy of citizens. As one congressman declared, "In my reading of history I recall no instance where a government perished because of the absence of a secret-service force, but many there are that perished as a result of the spy system."[10]

But Bonaparte was not deterred. He formed a new subdivision of the DOJ called the Bureau of Investigation, and brought in people from other agencies to staff it. In 1908 President Theodore Roosevelt issued an executive order authorizing the subdivision.

Table 1   Growth of the FBI

Year	Agents	Support Staff
1933	353	422
1945	4,380	7,422
2008	12,705	17,871

J. Edgar Hoover soon took the helm of the Bureau, which was re-named the FBI in 1935.[11]

Throughout the rest of the century, the FBI grew dramatically (see Table 1). During President Franklin Roosevelt's tenure, the size of the FBI increased more than 1000 percent.[12] It has continued to grow, tripling in size over the past sixty years.[13] Despite its vast size, extensive and expanding responsibilities, and profound technological capabilities, the FBI still lacks the congressional authorizing statute that most other federal agencies have.

The Growth of Electronic Surveillance

The FBI came into being as the debate over surveillance of communications entered a new era. Telephone wiretapping technology appeared soon after the invention of the telephone in 1876, making the privacy of phone communications a public concern. State legislatures responded by passing laws criminalizing wiretapping.

In 1928, in *Olmstead v. United States,* the U.S. Supreme Court held that the Fourth Amendment did not apply to wiretapping. "There was no searching," the Supreme Court reasoned. "There was no seizure. The evidence was secured by the use of the sense of hearing and that only. There was no entry of the houses or offices of the defendants."[14] Justice Louis Brandeis penned a powerful dissent, arguing that new technologies required rethinking old-fashioned notions of the Fourth Amendment: "Subtler and more far-reaching means of invading privacy have become available to the government. Discovery and invention have made it possible for the government, by means far more effective than stretching upon the rack, to obtain disclosure in court of what is whispered in the closet." He also mentioned that the Founders of the Constitution "conferred, as against the government, the right to be let alone—the most comprehensive of rights and the right most valued by civilized men. To protect that right, every unjustifiable intrusion by the government upon the privacy of the individual, whatever the means employed, must be deemed a violation of the Fourth Amendment."[15]

In 1934, six years after *Olmstead*, Congress passed a law to prohibit wiretapping.[16] But the law was largely ineffective, since it was interpreted only to preclude the introduction of wiretapping evidence in court.[17] The government could wiretap freely so long as it did not seek to use the product as evidence at trial.

During World War II and the ensuing Cold War, presidents gave the FBI new authorization to engage in wiretapping.[18] J. Edgar Hoover, still at the helm of the FBI, ordered wiretapping of hundreds of people, including dissidents, Supreme Court justices, professors, celebrities, writers, and others. Among Hoover's files were dossiers on John Steinbeck, Ernest Hemingway, Charlie Chaplin, Marlon Brando, Muhammad Ali, Albert Einstein, and numerous presidents and members of Congress.[19] When Justice William Douglas complained for years that the Supreme Court was being bugged and tapped, he seemed paranoid—but he was right.[20]

Protecting National Security: New Agencies and More Surveillance

During the 1940s and 1950s, enormous threats to national security loomed on the horizon. Concerns about the spread of communism and the Cold War with the Soviet Union led to an increased need for the government to engage in spying and foreign intelligence gathering. In 1942 President Roosevelt created the Office of Strategic Services (OSS) to engage in these activities, but it was eliminated after World War II. Just a few years later, however, President Truman revived the OSS's activities by creating the modern CIA with the National Security Act of 1947.

In 1952 Truman created the National Security Agency (NSA) to handle cryptology—the breaking of encryption codes so that any foreign communications collected could be analyzed. For a long time, the NSA operated with a low profile, and the few in the know quipped that its acronym stood for "No Such Agency."

Domestically, fears grew that communism was a threat not just from abroad but also from within. In the 1950s the FBI began the Counter Intelligence Program (COINTELPRO) to gather information about political groups viewed as national security threats. The FBI's tactics included secretly attempting to persuade employers to fire targeted individuals, anonymously informing spouses of affairs to break up marriages, and using the threat of Internal Revenue Service investigations to deter individuals from attending meetings and events.[21] The primary target was the American Communist Party, but by the late 1950s and early 1960s, COINTELPRO had expanded its interests to include members of the civil rights movement and opponents of the Vietnam War.[22] Included among these individuals was Martin Luther King, Jr., whom Hoover had under extensive surveillance. FBI recordings revealed that King was having extramarital affairs, and the FBI sent copies of the recordings to King and his wife, threatening that if King failed to commit suicide by a certain date, the recordings would be released publicly.[23]

The Criminal Procedure Revolution

In the 1960s the U.S. Supreme Court, led by Chief Justice Earl Warren, radically transformed criminal procedure. Police systems around the country had grown substantially, and the FBI and other federal law-enforcement agencies were increasingly active. There wasn't much law regulating how the government could go about collecting information about people.

To fill this void, the Supreme Court began boldly interpreting the Fourth and Fifth Amendments to regulate what law-enforcement officials could search and seize as well as how they could question suspects. In 1961, in *Mapp v. Ohio*, the Supreme Court held that evidence obtained in violation of the Fourth Amendment must be excluded from evidence in criminal trials.[24] In 1967 the Supreme Court overruled *Olmstead* in *United States v. Katz*, declaring that wiretapping was covered by the Fourth Amendment.[25] The Court articulated a broad test for the scope of Fourth Amendment protection — it would apply whenever the government violated a person's "reasonable expectation of privacy." In 1968, just a year after *Katz*, Congress enacted a law to better regulate electronic surveillance.[26] The law provided strict controls on government wiretapping and bugging.

Thus, through the efforts of the Supreme Court and Congress, legal regulation of government information gathering expanded significantly in the 1960s.

Regulating National Security Surveillance

An open question, however, existed for matters of national security. Were they to be treated differently from regular criminal investigations? In 1972 the U.S. Supreme Court addressed the question but didn't provide a definitive answer. It concluded that the Fourth Amendment applied to government surveillance for national security, though the rules to regulate it might differ from those involving ordinary crime.[27]

J. Edgar Hoover died in 1972, while still head of the FBI. He had been its director for nearly fifty years. Many presidents and members of Congress had feared Hoover and declined to take him on, but a few years after his death, Congress finally decided to take a closer look at the FBI, an inquiry spurred by the Watergate scandal and President Nixon's abuses of surveillance. Watergate involved electronic surveillance—the Watergate Office Building was burglarized in order to bug the phone of the Democratic Party chairman. Some of the charges in Nixon's impending impeachment involved misuse of officials at the FBI, the Secret Service, and other agencies to conduct electronic surveillance for improper purposes.

After Nixon resigned, on August 9, 1974, Congress realized that it needed to examine more thoroughly the way various government agencies were engaging in surveillance. Congress formed a special eleven-member committee in 1975 to investigate surveillance abuses over the previous forty years.[28] Led by Senator Frank Church, the committee published fourteen volumes of reports and supporting documents. The Church Committee concluded that the government had engaged in numerous abuses of surveillance, often targeting people solely because of their political beliefs. Specifically, the committee declared: "Too many people have been spied upon by too many Government agencies and [too] much information has [been] collected. The Government has often undertaken the secret surveillance of citizens on the basis of their political beliefs, even when those beliefs posed no threat of violence or illegal acts on behalf of a hostile foreign power."[29] As the committee noted, every president from Franklin Roosevelt to Richard Nixon improperly used government surveillance to obtain information about critics and political opponents.[30]

In part as a response to shocking findings of the Church Committee Report, Congress passed the Foreign Intelligence Surveillance Act (FISA) in 1978.[31] The purpose of FISA was to erect a "secure framework by which the executive branch could conduct legitimate electronic surveillance for foreign intelligence purposes within the context of this Nation's commitment to privacy and individual rights."[32] Additionally, the attorney general established a set of guidelines for FBI investigations in 1976.[33] Moreover, major reforms were instituted at the FBI to prevent the kinds of abuses that had occurred during Hoover's reign as director. The FBI director was limited to a term of no longer than ten years.

Receding Fourth Amendment Protection and the Rise of the Information Age

In the 1970s and 1980s the Supreme Court issued several decisions narrowing the scope of Fourth Amendment protection. For example, the Court concluded that there was no reasonable expectation of privacy when the police obtained a list of the phone numbers a person dialed or gathered a person's bank records or peered down on a person's property from a helicopter or rummaged through a person's trash left out for collection.[34]

During the 1990s the rise of computers, the burgeoning use of the Internet and email, and the increasing use of digital records began to pose severe challenges for the federal wiretap statute, which had not been created with these new technologies in mind. In anticipation of the increasing use of computers, Congress updated its electronic surveillance law in 1986 with a statute called the Electronic Communications Privacy Act (ECPA).[35] This law aimed to provide protection of email, stored computer files, and communications records. Unfortunately, the law has not been dramatically restructured since its passage. Changes have been made here and there, but the ECPA remains largely the same. A quarter of a century after its passage, it has gone far out of date.

The War on Terrorism

Then came the terrorist attacks of September 11, 2001. We became aware of dangerous terrorist cells within our borders. In an extremely short time following the September 11 attacks, Congress passed the USA Patriot Act of 2001, which made a series of updates to ECPA and FISA, generally giving the government greater power to engage in surveillance.[36] To better facilitate information sharing among the various federal agencies, many agencies were merged into DHS.

Throughout this time, the government engaged in many clandestine information-gathering programs. The NSA began wiretapping phone calls between U.S. citizens and people abroad. Various federal agencies collected records from airlines and other businesses for use in data mining.

Privacy, Security, and the Law

Throughout the past century, as we moved into the Information Age, the government has expanded its arsenal of techniques to protect security. Law enforcement in the past mostly involved searches of homes, people, and papers. Now the government uses technology to gather records and data, to engage in audio and visual surveillance, and to track movement. Much law-enforcement activity with implications for privacy involves "information gathering." I'll use this term broadly to encompass the wide variety of ways the government can find out what people are doing, thinking, or planning. In addition to gathering information, the government also stores it, uses it, analyzes it, combines it, and sometimes discloses it. All these activities can threaten privacy.

As the history I have sketched illustrates, the law has responded in many ways to the clash between privacy and security. Today the government has tremendous power and technological capabilities to enforce the law and promote security. The law establishes privacy protections to ensure that the government doesn't abuse its power. The Fourth Amendment to the U.S. Constitution is the primary form of regulation of government information gathering.

Under our system of law, the Constitution provides the minimum level of privacy protection. A state can't provide any less protection. Nor can a federal statute. Other amendments, such as the Fifth and (as I'll argue later) the First, protect some dimensions of privacy.

In addition to the Constitution, several federal laws regulate certain forms of government information gathering. ECPA regulates wiretapping, bugging, and searches of computers, among other things. FISA regulates foreign intelligence gathering on foreign agents on U.S. soil. Other statutes provide some regulation of government access to our records, such as cable or health records.

There are also state constitutional protections of privacy and state statutes. These can supply additional privacy protections, though they restrict only police departments within a particular state. They can't limit FBI agents or any other federal law-enforcement officials even when they're acting within the state. Federal agents are limited only by the U.S. Constitution and federal statutes. In this book, my focus will be almost entirely on the U.S. Constitution and federal law.

Does the law provide a good balance between privacy and security? I believe the answer is no. Lessons learned after previous surveillance abuses have been forgotten. Protections put into the law in response to these abuses have been removed. I'll explain how the law regulating privacy and security works, point out its failings, and suggest how it can be improved.

A Roadmap

In this book I shall explore four general issues, and I have organized it accordingly, devoting the four parts to (1) *values*—how we should assess and balance the values of privacy and security; (2) *times of crisis*—how the law should address matters of national security; (3) *constitutional rights*—how the Constitution should protect privacy; and (4) *new technologies*—how the law should cope with changing technology.

Within each part are chapters exploring various subtopics. You can read chapters independently of one another.

Values

Part I involves the values of privacy and security. How should we assess and understand these values? Can they be reconciled? How should we balance them when they conflict? The chapters in this part are concerned with how we can better understand what privacy protection entails, how we can more thoughtfully evaluate the costs and benefits of security measures, and how we can balance privacy and security in a way that isn't skewed too much toward security. Privacy is often misunderstood and undervalued when balanced against security. It is possible to have potent security measures and to protect privacy too, since protecting privacy doesn't entail scrapping security measures but demands only that they be subjected to oversight and regulation.

In Chapter 2 I examine the "nothing-to-hide argument." Those making this common argument contend that they have nothing to hide from the government. I demonstrate why this argument is faulty.

Chapter 3 tackles another argument, that in order to increase security, we must sacrifice privacy. I call this the "all-or-nothing fallacy" because it falsely assumes that privacy and security are mutually exclusive.

In Chapter 4 I explore the "deference argument"—that we should be careful about second-guessing the judgments of security officials because they have more expertise in dealing with national security than judges or legislators. Courts often defer to security officials, and I argue that this deference unduly skews the balance between privacy rights and security.

In Chapter 5 I argue that privacy isn't merely an individual right. The balancing between security and privacy is often conducted improperly because the security interest is characterized as beneficial for all society while the privacy interest is viewed as a particular individual's concern. I contend that privacy should be understood as a societal value.

Times of Crisis

In Part II I examine the law during periods of crisis. When we're facing a threat to national security, the government frequently curtails rights, circumvents laws, and demands greater discretion, more secrecy, and less oversight. The chapters in this part demonstrate that these special powers and exceptions to the rule of law are often unnecessary and wrongheaded.

In Chapter 6 I address the "pendulum argument"—that in times of crisis, we must sacrifice some liberties, which will be restored when the crisis is over. I contend that this argument has it exactly backward. In times of crisis, we should be at our staunchest in protecting liberty.

In Chapter 7 I critique the "national security argument"—that government information gathering about U.S. citizens in the name of national security should be subjected to less regulation and oversight than the investigation of ordinary crime. I argue that the distinction between matters of national security and regular crime is fuzzy and incoherent.

In Chapter 8 I discuss the importance of "crime-espionage distinction"—separating the rules regulating criminal investigation from the rules regulating espionage. After September 11, the distinction was significantly dissolved. I argue that the distinction must be kept intact.

In Chapter 9 I examine how law protecting privacy and other civil liberties is often violated in times of crisis. A prime example was the NSA surveillance program, under which the NSA contravened the law by engaging in warrantless wiretapping of phone calls. If we can't ensure that the law is followed, the rule of law becomes meaningless.

Constitutional Rights

Part III focuses on constitutional rights. What do our constitutional rights entail? How do they protect us? Frequently, people think that constitutional rights protect a lot more than they actually do. As I explain in this part, numerous government information-gathering activities are completely unregulated. If the Constitution is to provide for meaningful regulation and oversight of government data gathering in the Information Age, then the Supreme Court's interpretations of the Constitution need a radical overhaul.

In Chapter 10 I discuss the latest tools of government information gathering, many of which aren't restricted by the Fourth Amendment. The scope of Fourth Amendment regulation, which depends on whether the government violates privacy, is unduly constrained because the U.S. Supreme Court understands privacy as a form of total secrecy. I call this view of privacy the "secrecy paradigm," and I demonstrate that it is antiquated and flawed.

In Chapter 11 I analyze the "third party doctrine," which holds that whenever a person or business exposes information to another entity, no reasonable expectation of privacy remains, and thus no Fourth Amendment protection applies. In the Information Age, however, an unprecedented amount of personal data is in the hands of third parties, effectively removing Fourth Amendment protection from it.

In Chapter 12 I argue that Fourth Amendment law needs dramatic reform. In many cases, government activities are unregulated because the Supreme Court doesn't think "privacy" is involved. I propose that paradoxically, Fourth Amendment law would do a better job of protecting privacy by no longer focusing on privacy.

In Chapter 13 I explain the "suspicionless-searches" argument, which contends that requiring law enforcements to establish suspicion before engaging in a search isn't compatible with efforts to prevent terrorism. I show that abandoning the suspicion requirement—as embodied in warrants and probable cause—provides law-enforcement officials with too much power and discretion and too little oversight.

In Chapter 14 I examine whether the exclusionary rule—which makes evidence gathered in violation of the Fourth Amendment unusable at trial—is an appropriate remedy, especially when a heinous crime or terrorist act is involved. I discuss how the Fourth Amendment can be enforced without the exclusionary rule.

In Chapter 15 I argue that the First Amendment should protect you when the government seeks information about your speech, association, beliefs, or reading habits.

New Technologies

Part IV is concerned with the challenges that new technologies pose for the law. How should the law cope in a world of rapidly changing technology? In this part I examine the ways statutory law regulates government information gathering and the difficulty of keeping statutes up-to-date. The best way to protect privacy is never to lose sight of general principles. To avoid becoming outmoded when the technology evolves, laws should be built around general principles rather than specific technologies.

In Chapter 16 I focus on the Patriot Act, a law many argue should be repealed. But what if the Patriot Act were to simply disappear tomorrow? Contrary to the conventional wisdom, little would change.

In Chapter 17 I critique the "leave-it-to-the-legislature argument"—that legislatures are better than courts at making the rules when new technologies are involved. I argue that courts must remain actively involved in order to ensure that the law keeps up with new technology.

In Chapter 18 I examine government data mining—the use of databases of personal information to analyze for patterns to determine who is acting suspiciously. Currently, the Fourth Amendment does not do much to protect against data mining. I distinguish between when the government should be allowed to engage in data mining and when it shouldn't.

In Chapter 19 I argue that the law doesn't adequately regulate public video surveillance. In the United Kingdom millions of surveillance cameras watch everything people do. Such a system could readily be implemented in America—and it currently is being implemented in various cities. I explain how the law can provide better regulation.

In Chapter 20 I critique the "Luddite argument"—that opposition to new security technologies (such as biometric identification) stems from an aversion to new technology. I argue that concerns about these technologies are often legitimate. While many of the technologies offer great upsides, they can have catastrophic consequences if they fail.

P A R T I

Values

How We Should Assess and Balance the

Values of Privacy and Security

The Nothing-to-Hide Argument

When the government gathers or analyzes personal information, many people say they're not worried. "I've got nothing
to hide," they declare. "Only if you're doing something wrong
should you worry, and then you don't deserve to keep it private."

The nothing-to-hide argument pervades discussions about
privacy. The data security expert Bruce Schneier calls it the "most
common retort against privacy advocates."[1] The legal scholar Geoffrey Stone refers to it as an "all-too-common refrain."[2] In its most
compelling form, it is an argument that the privacy interest is generally minimal, thus making the balance against security concerns a
foreordained victory for security. In this chapter, I'll demonstrate how
the argument stems from certain faulty assumptions about privacy and
its value.

"I've Got Nothing to Hide"

The nothing-to-hide argument is everywhere. In Britain, for example,
the government has installed millions of public surveillance cameras
in cities and towns, which are watched by officials via closed-circuit
television. In a campaign slogan for the program, the government

declares: "If you've got nothing to hide, you've got nothing to fear."[3] In the United States, one anonymous individual comments: "If [government officials] need to read my e-mails . . . so be it. I have nothing to hide. Do you?"[4] Variations of nothing-to-hide arguments frequently appear in blogs, letters to the editor, television news interviews, and other forums. One blogger, in reference to profiling people for national security purposes, declares: "Go ahead and profile me, I have nothing to hide."[5] Another blogger proclaims: "So I don't mind people wanting to find out things about me, I've got nothing to hide! Which is why I support [the government's] efforts to find terrorists by monitoring our phone calls!"[6] Some other examples include:

- I don't have anything to hide from the government. I don't think I had that much hidden from the government in the first place. I don't think they care if I talk about my ornery neighbor.[7]

- Do I care if the FBI monitors my phone calls? I have nothing to hide. Neither does 99.99 percent of the population. If the wiretapping stops one of these Sept. 11 incidents, thousands of lives are saved.[8]

- Like I said, I have nothing to hide. The majority of the American people have nothing to hide. And those that have something to hide should be found out, and get what they have coming to them.[9]

The nothing-to-hide argument is not of recent vintage. One of the characters in Henry James's 1888 novel *The Reverberator* muses: "If these people had done bad things they ought to be ashamed of themselves and he couldn't pity them, and if they hadn't done them there was no need of making such a rumpus about other people knowing."[10]

I encountered the nothing-to-hide argument so frequently in news interviews, discussions, and the like that I decided to probe the issue. I asked the readers of my blog, *Concurring Opinions*, whether there are good responses to the nothing-to-hide argument.[11] I received a torrent of comments:

- My response is "So do you have curtains?" or "Can I see your credit card bills for the last year?"
- So my response to the "If you have nothing to hide . . . " argument is simply, "I don't need to justify my position. You need to justify yours. Come back with a warrant."
- I don't have anything to hide. But I don't have anything I feel like showing you, either.
- If you have nothing to hide, then you don't have a life.
- Show me yours and I'll show you mine.
- It's not about having anything to hide, it's about things not being anyone else's business.
- Bottom line, Joe Stalin would [have] loved it. Why should anyone have to say more?[12]

On the surface it seems easy to dismiss the nothing-to-hide argument. Everybody probably has something to hide from somebody. As the author Aleksandr Solzhenitsyn declared, "Everyone is guilty of something or has something to conceal. All one has to do is look hard enough to find what it is."[13] Likewise, in Friedrich Dürrenmatt's novella *Traps*, which involves a seemingly innocent man put on trial by a group of retired lawyers for a mock trial game, the man inquires what his crime shall be. "'An altogether minor matter,' the prosecutor replied. . . . 'A crime can always be found.'"[14]

One can usually think of something that even the most open person would want to hide. As a commenter to my blog post noted, "If you have nothing to hide, then that quite literally means you are willing to let me photograph you naked? And I get full rights to that photograph—so I can show it to your neighbors?"[15] The Canadian privacy expert David Flaherty expresses a similar idea when he argues: "There is no sentient human being in the Western world who has little or no regard for his or her personal privacy; those who would attempt such claims cannot withstand even a few minutes' questioning about intimate aspects of their lives without capitulating to the intrusiveness of certain subject matters."[16]

Such responses attack the nothing-to-hide argument only in its most extreme form, which isn't particularly strong. In a less extreme form, the nothing-to-hide argument refers not to all personal information but only to the type of data the government is likely to collect. Retorts to the nothing-to-hide argument about exposing people's naked bodies or their deepest secrets are relevant only if the government is likely to gather this kind of information. In many instances, hardly anyone will see the information, and it won't be disclosed to the public. Thus, some might argue, the privacy interest is minimal, and the security interest in preventing terrorism is much more important. In this less extreme form, the nothing-to-hide argument is a formidable one.

Understanding Privacy

To evaluate the nothing-to-hide argument, we should begin by looking at how its adherents understand privacy. Nearly every law or policy involving privacy depends upon a particular understanding of what privacy is. The way problems are conceived has a tremendous impact on the legal and policy solutions used to solve them. As the philosopher John Dewey observed, "A problem well put is half-solved."[17]

What is "privacy"? Most attempts to understand privacy do so by attempting to locate the essence of privacy—its core characteristics or the common denominator that links together the various things we classify under the rubric of "privacy." Privacy, however, is too complex a concept to be reduced to a singular essence. It is a plurality of different things that do not share one element in common but that nevertheless bear a resemblance to each other.[18] For example, privacy can be invaded by the disclosure of your deepest secrets. It might also be invaded if you're watched by a Peeping Tom, even if no secrets are ever revealed to anyone. With the disclosure of secrets, the harm is that your concealed information is spread to others. With the Peeping Tom, the harm is that you're being watched. You'd probably find it creepy regardless of whether the peeper finds out anything sensitive or discloses any information to others.

There are many other forms of invasion of privacy, such as blackmail or the improper use of your personal data. Your privacy can also be invaded if the government compiles an extensive dossier about you. Privacy thus involves so many different things that it is impossible to reduce them all to one simple idea. We need not do so.

In many cases, privacy issues never get balanced against conflicting interests because courts, legislators, and others fail to recognize that privacy is implicated. People don't acknowledge certain problems because they don't fit into their particular one-size-fits-all conception of privacy. Regardless of whether we call something a "privacy" problem, it still remains a problem, and problems shouldn't be ignored. We should pay attention to all the different problems that spark our desire to protect privacy.

To describe the problems created by the collection and use of personal data, many commentators use a metaphor based on George Orwell's *Nineteen Eighty-Four*.[19] Orwell depicted a harrowing totalitarian society ruled by a government called Big Brother that watched its citizens obsessively and demanded strict discipline. The Orwell metaphor, which focuses on the harms of surveillance (such as inhibition and social control), might be apt to describe government monitoring of citizens. But much of the data gathered in computer databases isn't particularly sensitive, such as one's race, birth date, gender, address, or marital status. Many people don't care about concealing the hotels they stay at, the cars they own, or the kind of beverages they drink. Frequently, though not always, people wouldn't be inhibited or embarrassed if others knew this information.

A different metaphor better captures the problems: Franz Kafka's *The Trial*. Kafka's novel centers around a man who is arrested but not informed why. He desperately tries to find out what triggered his arrest and what's in store for him. He finds out that a mysterious court system has a dossier on him and is investigating him, but he's unable to learn much more. *The Trial* depicts a bureaucracy with inscrutable purposes that uses people's information to make important decisions about them, yet denies the people the ability to participate in how their information is used.[20] The problems portrayed by the Kafkaesque metaphor are of a different sort from the problems caused by surveillance. They often do not result in inhibition. Instead, they are problems of information processing—the storage, use, or analysis of data—rather than of information collection. They affect the power relationships between people and the institutions of the modern state. They not only frustrate the individual by creating a sense of helplessness and powerlessness, they also affect social structure by altering the kind of relationships people have with the institutions that make important decisions about their lives.

Legal and policy solutions focus too much on the problems under the Orwellian metaphor—those of surveillance—and aren't adequately addressing the Kafkaesque problems—those of information processing.[21] The difficulty is that commentators are trying to conceive of the problems caused by databases in terms of surveillance when, in fact, these problems are different.

The Problem with the Nothing-to-Hide Argument

Commentators often attempt to refute the nothing-to-hide argument by pointing to things people want to hide. But the problem with the nothing-to-hide argument is the underlying assumption that privacy is about hiding bad things. By accepting this assumption we concede far too much ground and invite an unproductive discussion of information people would likely want to hide. As Bruce Schneier aptly notes, the nothing-to-hide argument stems from a faulty "premise that privacy is about hiding a wrong."[22] Surveillance, for example, can inhibit such lawful activities as free speech, free association, and other First Amendment rights essential for democracy.

The deeper problem with the nothing-to-hide argument is that it myopically views privacy as a form of secrecy. In contrast, understanding privacy as a plurality of related issues demonstrates that the disclosure of bad things is just one among many difficulties caused by government security measures. To return to my discussion of literary metaphors, the problems are not just Orwellian but Kafkaesque. Government information-gathering programs are problematic even if no information people want to hide is uncovered. In *The Trial*, the problem is not inhibited behavior but rather a suffocating powerlessness and vulnerability created by the court system's use of personal data and its denial to the protagonist of any knowledge of or participation in the process. The harms are bureaucratic ones—indifference, error, abuse, frustration, and lack of transparency and accountability.

One such harm, for example, which I call *aggregation*, emerges from the fusion of small bits of seemingly innocuous data. When combined, the information becomes much more telling. By joining pieces of information we might not take pains to guard, the government can glean information about us that we might indeed wish to conceal. For example, suppose you bought a book about cancer. This purchase isn't very revealing on its own, for it just indicates an interest in the disease. Suppose you bought a wig. The purchase of a wig, by itself, could be for a number of reasons. But combine these two pieces of information, and now the inference can be made that you have cancer and are undergoing chemotherapy.

Another potential problem with the government's harvest of personal data is one I call *exclusion*. Exclusion occurs when people are prevented from having knowledge about how information about them is being used, and when they are barred from accessing and correcting errors in that data. Many government national security measures involve maintaining a massive database of information that individuals cannot access. Indeed, because they involve national security, the very existence of these programs is often kept secret. This kind of information processing, which blocks subjects' knowledge and involvement, resembles in some ways a kind of due-process problem. It is a structural problem involving the way people are treated by government institutions and creating a power imbalance between individuals and the government. To what extent should government officials have such a significant power over citizens? This issue isn't about what information people want to hide but about the power and the structure of government.

A related problem involves *secondary use*. Secondary use is the exploitation of data obtained for one purpose for an unrelated purpose without the subject's consent. How long will personal data be stored? How will it be used? What could it be used for in the future? The potential future uses of any piece of personal information are vast, and without limits on or accountability for how that information is used, it is hard for people to assess the dangers of the data's being in the government's control.

Yet another problem with government gathering and use of personal data is *distortion*. Although personal information can reveal quite a lot about people's personalities and activities, it often fails to reflect the whole person. It can paint a distorted picture, especially since records are reductive—they often capture information in a standardized format with many details omitted.

For example, suppose government officials learn that a person has bought a number of books on how to manufacture methamphetamine. That information makes them suspect that he's building a meth lab. What is missing from the records is the full story: The person is writing a novel about a character who makes meth. When he bought the books, he didn't consider how suspicious the purchase might appear to government officials, and his records didn't reveal the reason for the purchases. Should he have to worry about government scrutiny of all his purchases and actions? Should he have to be concerned that he'll wind up on a suspicious-persons list? Even if he isn't doing anything wrong, he may want to keep his records away from government officials who might make faulty inferences from them. He might not want to have to worry about how everything he does will be perceived by officials nervously monitoring for criminal activity. He might not want to have a computer flag him as suspicious because he has an unusual pattern of behavior.

The problem with the nothing-to-hide argument is that it focuses on just one or two particular kinds of privacy problems—the disclosure of personal information or surveillance—while ignoring others. It assumes a particular view about what privacy entails to the exclusion of other perspectives.

It is important to distinguish here between two ways of justifying a national security program that demands access to personal information. The first way is not to recognize a problem. This is how the nothing-to-hide argument works—it denies even the existence of a problem. The second manner of justifying such a program is to acknowledge the problems but contend that the benefits of the program outweigh the privacy sacrifice. The first justification influences the second, because the low value given to privacy is based upon a narrow view of the problem. The key misunderstanding is that the nothing-to-hide argument views privacy in a particular way—as a form of secrecy, as the right to hide things. But there are many other types of harm involved beyond exposing one's secrets to the government.

Blood, Death, and Privacy

One of the difficulties with the nothing-to-hide argument is that it looks for a singular and visceral kind of injury. Ironically, this underlying conception of injury is sometimes shared by those advocating for greater privacy protections. For example, the law professor Ann Bartow argues that in order to have a real resonance, privacy problems must "negatively impact the lives of living, breathing human beings beyond simply provoking feelings of unease." She urges that privacy needs more "dead bodies" and that privacy's "lack of blood and death, or at least of broken bones and buckets of money, distances privacy harms from other [types of harm]."[23]

Bartow's objection is actually consistent with the nothing-to-hide argument. Those advancing the nothing-to-hide argument have in mind a particular kind of appalling privacy harm, one where privacy is violated only when something deeply embarrassing or discrediting is revealed. Like Bartow, proponents of the nothing-to-hide argument demand a dead-bodies type of harm.

Bartow is certainly right that people respond much more strongly to blood and death than to more abstract concerns. But if this is the standard to recognize a problem, then few privacy problems will be recognized. Privacy is not a horror movie, most privacy problems don't result in dead bodies, and demanding more palpable harms will be difficult in many cases.

In many instances, privacy is threatened not by a single egregious act but by the accretion of a slow series of relatively minor acts. In this respect, privacy problems resemble certain environmental harms which occur over time through a series of small acts by different actors. Although society is more likely to respond to a major oil spill, gradual pollution by a multitude of different actors often creates worse problems.

Privacy is rarely lost in one fell swoop. It is often eroded over time, little bits dissolving almost imperceptibly until we finally begin to notice how much is gone. When the government starts monitoring the phone numbers people call, many may shrug their shoulders and say, "Ah, it's just numbers, that's all." Then the government might start monitoring some phone calls. "It's just a few phone calls, nothing more," people might declare. The government might install more video cameras in public places, to which some would respond, "So what? Some more cameras watching in a few more places. No big deal." The increase in cameras might ultimately expand to a more elaborate network of video surveillance. Satellite surveillance might be added, as well as the tracking of people's movements. The government might start analyzing people's bank records. "It's just my deposits and some of the bills I pay—no problem." The government may then start combing through credit card records, then expand to Internet service provider (ISP) records, health records, employment records, and more. Each step may seem incremental, but after a while, the government will be watching and knowing everything about us.

"My life's an open book," people might say. "I've got nothing to hide." But now the government has a massive dossier of everyone's activities, interests, reading habits, finances, and health. What if the government leaks the information to the public? What if the government mistakenly determines that based on your pattern of activities, you're likely to engage in a criminal act? What if it denies you the right to fly? What if the government thinks your financial transactions look odd—even if you've done nothing wrong—and freezes your accounts? What if the government doesn't protect your information with adequate security, and an identity thief obtains it and uses it to defraud you? Even if you have nothing to hide, the government can cause you a lot of harm.

"But the government doesn't want to hurt me," some might argue. In many cases, this is true, but the government can also harm people inadvertently, due to errors or carelessness.

Silencing the Nothing-to-Hide Argument

When the nothing-to-hide argument is unpacked, and its underlying assumptions examined and challenged, we can see how it shifts the debate to its terms, then draws power from its unfair advantage. The nothing-to-hide argument speaks to some problems, but not to others. It represents a singular and narrow way of conceiving of privacy, and it wins by excluding consideration of the other problems often raised with government security measures. When engaged directly, the nothing-to-hide argument can ensnare, for it forces the debate to focus on its narrow understanding of privacy. But when confronted with the plurality of privacy problems implicated by government data collection and use beyond surveillance and disclosure, the nothing-to-hide argument, in the end, has nothing to say.

The All-or-Nothing Fallacy

"**I**'d gladly give up my privacy if it will keep me secure from a terrorist attack." I hear this refrain again and again. The debate is often cast as an all-or-nothing choice, whether we should have privacy or a specific security measure. Consider the way the government defended the NSA surveillance program, which involved secret wiretapping of phone calls without any oversight. In a congressional hearing, Attorney General Alberto Gonzales stated: "Our enemy is listening, and I cannot help but wonder if they are not shaking their heads in amazement at the thought that anyone would imperil such a sensitive program by leaking its existence in the first place, and smiling at the prospect that we might now disclose even more or perhaps even unilaterally disarm ourselves of a key tool in the war on terror."[1]

Notice his language. He's implying that if we protect privacy, it will mean that we must "disarm" ourselves of some really valuable security measures. He's suggesting that even terrorists would consider us crazy for making such a tradeoff.

I constantly hear arguments like this when officials justify security measures or argue that they shouldn't be regulated. They point to the value of the surveillance and the peril we'd be in without it. "We're hearing quite a lot of chatter about terrorist attacks," they say.

"Do you want us to stop listening? Then the terrorists could talk about how they plan to blow up a plane, and we won't know about it. Is a little privacy really worth that cost?"

Those defending the national-security side of the balance often view security and liberty as a zero-sum tradeoff. The legal scholars Eric Posner and Adrian Vermeule contend that "any increase in security requires a decrease in liberty."[2] The argument is that security and civil liberties such as privacy can never be reconciled. Every gain in privacy must be a loss in security. Every gain in security must be a loss in privacy.

But this argument is flawed. The argument that privacy and security are mutually exclusive stems from what I call the "all-or-nothing fallacy." Sacrificing privacy doesn't automatically make us more secure. Not all security measures are invasive of privacy. Moreover, no correlation has been established between the effectiveness of a security measure and a corresponding decrease in liberty. In other words, the most effective security measures need not be the most detrimental to liberty.

So common is the all-or-nothing fallacy that many people feel safer the more the government invades their privacy. I think of the fallacy as the reaction of people on a sinking boat in the middle of the ocean. Frantic to stay afloat, the passengers start throwing all sorts of things overboard. They think: *If we toss stuff overboard, then we'll stop sinking.* But in their fear, they throw away a chest of food and water. Meanwhile, the boat was sinking because of a hole that could have easily been plugged.

Security and privacy need not be mutually exclusive. For example, one security response to the September 11 attacks was to lock the cockpit doors on airplanes. This prevents a terrorist from gaining control of the plane. Does it invade privacy? Hardly at all. Chasing down unaccounted-for nuclear weapons abroad is another security measure that often isn't invasive of privacy.

I think one reason for the prevalence of the all-or-nothing fallacy is that people seem to associate being inconvenienced and being intruded upon with security. So if the government wants to make people feel more secure, all it needs to do is make them feel more uncomfortable and exposed. But surrendering privacy doesn't necessarily make us more secure.

The all-or-nothing fallacy causes tremendous distortion in the balance between privacy and security. In fact, I believe that many courts and commentators who balance security measures against privacy rights conduct the balance wrongly because of this fallacy. They cast the balance in terms of whether a particular government security measure should be barred. On one side of the scale they weigh the benefits of the security measure. On the other side they weigh privacy rights.

At first blush, this seems like a reasonable approach—balance the security measure against privacy. Yet it is quite wrong. Placing the security measure on the scale assumes that the *entire security measure, all-or-nothing, is in the balance.* It's not. Protecting privacy seldom negates the security measure altogether. Rarely does judicial oversight or the application of the Fourth Amendment prohibit a government surveillance activity. Instead, the activity is allowed subject to oversight and sometimes a degree of limitation.

Most constitutional and statutory protections work this way. The Fourth Amendment, for example, allows all sorts of very invasive searches. Under the Fourth Amendment, the government can search your home. It can search your computer. It can do a full body-cavity search. It can search nearly anything and engage in nearly any kind of surveillance. How can this be so? Because the Fourth Amendment doesn't protect privacy by stopping the government from searching; it works by requiring judicial oversight and mandating that the government justify its measures. So under the Fourth Amendment, the government can engage in highly invasive searches if it justifies the need to do so beforehand to a judge.

Like the Fourth Amendment, electronic-surveillance law allows for wiretapping, but limits the practice by mandating judicial supervision, minimizing the breadth of the wiretapping, and requiring law-enforcement officials to report back to the court to prevent abuses. Thus the protection of privacy might demand the imposition of oversight and regulation but need not entail scrapping an entire security measure.

When security is balanced against privacy, the entire security measure shouldn't be weighed against the privacy harms it creates. Since protecting privacy involves imposing oversight and regulation on the initiative, the security side of the scale should gauge only the extent to which such oversight and regulation reduce the effectiveness of the security measure. If, say, judicial oversight and regulation designed to protect privacy result in delays and paperwork and limitations that make a security measure 10 percent less effective, it makes no sense to balance the entire security measure against privacy. Instead, the balance should be between privacy and the 10 percent decrease in the measure's effectiveness.

Far too often, however, discussions of security and liberty fail to assess the balance this way. Polls frequently pose the question as an all-or-nothing tradeoff. A 2002 Pew Research poll asked American citizens:

> Should the government be allowed to read e-mails and listen to phone calls to fight terrorism?[3]

A 2005 poll from Rasmussen Reports posed the question:

> Should the National Security Agency be allowed to intercept telephone conversations between terrorism suspects in other countries and people living in the United States?[4]

Both these questions, however, neglect to account for warrants and court orders. Few would contend that the government shouldn't be allowed to conduct a wide range of searches when it has a search warrant or court order. So the questions that *should* be posed are:

Should the government be allowed to read emails and listen to phone calls *without a search warrant or the appropriate court order required by law* to fight terrorism?

Should the National Security Agency be allowed to intercept telephone conversations between terrorism suspects in other countries and people living in the United States *without a court order or judicial oversight?*

The choice is not between a security measure and nothing, but between a security measure with oversight and regulation and a security measure at the sole discretion of executive officials. In many cases, oversight and regulation do not diminish a security measure substantially, so the cost of protecting privacy can be quite low. Unfortunately, the balance is rarely assessed properly. When the balance is measured under the all-or-nothing fallacy, the scale dips dramatically toward the security side. The costs of protecting privacy are falsely inflated, and the security measure is accorded too much weight.

4

The Danger of Deference

A fter the London subway bombing in 2005, New York City officials began to worry about the possibility of a similar attack in New York. The New York Police Department began a program of random searches of riders' baggage. The searches were conducted without a warrant, probable cause, or even reasonable suspicion.

The search program was challenged as a violation of the Fourth Amendment. The Fourth Amendment allows random searches if they are "reasonable," a quality that is determined by balancing the government interest in security against people's interest in privacy. The weight of the security interest depends upon the extent to which the program effectively improves subway safety. Nobody questions the importance of subway safety, so the critical issue is whether the search program is a sufficiently effective way of achieving security to be worth the tradeoff in privacy and civil liberties.

In *MacWade v. Kelly*, the U.S. Court of Appeals for the Second Circuit conducted this balancing act and concluded that the program was reasonable under the Fourth Amendment. The way the court conducted this analysis, however, was problematic. On the issue of the effectiveness of the subway search program, the court deferred to the law-enforcement officials, stating that the issue "is best left to those with a unique understanding of, and responsibility for, limited public resources, including a finite number of police officers." In determining whether the program was "a reasonably effective means of addressing the government interest in deterring and detecting a terrorist attack on the subway system," the court refused to examine the data to assess the program's effectiveness. The court declared:

> We will not peruse, parse, or extrapolate four months' worth of data in an attempt to divine how many checkpoints the City ought to deploy in the exercise of its day-to-day police power. Counterterrorism experts and politically accountable officials have undertaken the delicate and esoteric task of deciding how best to marshal their available resources in light of the conditions prevailing on any given day. We will not—and *may not*—second-guess the minutiae of their considered decisions.[1]

Was the New York subway search program effective? I doubt it. About 4.5 million passengers ride on New York subways every weekday, and the city has more than 450 subway stations.[2] A small number of random searches seems more symbolic than effective because the odds of the police finding terrorists are very low.

Under the program, a person can walk away rather than be searched. Any terrorist who isn't foolish would leave the station and walk about ten blocks to another station, where searches probably wouldn't be occurring, since searching is limited to a few stations each day.

The government argued that the program would deter terrorists from bringing bombs onto subway trains. But nearly any kind of security measure can arguably produce some degree of deterrence. The key issue, which the court didn't analyze, is whether the program would lead to deterrence significant enough to outweigh the curtailment of civil liberties.

Deference is a major problem when it comes to balancing security and privacy. Although courts should not take a know-it-all attitude, they shouldn't defer on such a critical question as a security measure's effectiveness. The problem with many security measures is that they are not wise expenditures of resources. In addition, they have costs in terms of people's privacy and civil liberties. Holding them up to the bright light and scrutinizing them is a way to make sure they are truly effective enough to be worth the costs. Many courts, however, are reluctant to second-guess the judgment of security experts. In this chapter, I argue that courts should not defer to the government's security experts.

Does the Executive Branch Have Greater Competence in Security?

Judge Richard Posner argues that judges should defer to the executive branch when it comes to assessing security measures because judges "aren't *supposed* to know much about national security."[3] Likewise, his son Eric Posner, joined by fellow legal scholar Adrian Vermeule, declares that "the executive branch, not Congress or the judicial branch, should make the tradeoff between security and liberty."[4]

The problem with deference is that, historically, the executive branch hasn't always made the wisest national security decisions. Nonetheless, Posner and Vermeule contend that notwithstanding its mistakes, the executive branch is better at making these decisions than are the judicial and legislative branches. "Judges are generalists," they observe, "and the political insulation that protects them from current politics also deprives them of information, especially information about novel security threats and necessary responses to those threats." Posner and Vermeule argue that during emergencies, the "novelty of the threats and of the necessary responses makes judicial routines and evolved legal rules seem inapposite, even obstructive."[5]

"Judicial routines" and "legal rules," however, make up the cornerstone of due process and the rule of law—they are the central building blocks of a free and democratic society. At many times, Posner, Vermeule, and other strong proponents of security seem to focus almost exclusively on what would be best for security. But the objective should be establishing an optimal balance between security and liberty. Although such a balance may not promote security with maximum efficiency, that is one of the costs of living in a democracy as opposed to an authoritarian political regime. The executive branch may be the appropriate branch for developing security measures, but that does not make it the most adept branch at establishing a balance between security and liberty.

In our constitutional democracy, each branch has a role to play in making policy. Courts protect constitutional rights, not as absolute restrictions on executive and legislative policymaking but as important interests to be balanced against government interests. Judges balance by applying various forms of "judicial scrutiny," which involve assessing the weight of the government's interest, a particular measure's effectiveness in protecting that interest, and the extent to which the government interest can be achieved without unduly infringing upon constitutional rights. For balancing to be meaningful, courts must scrutinize both the security and the liberty interests.

If courts fail to question the efficacy of security measures, then the security interest will prevail nearly all the time. Preventing terrorism has an immensely heavy weight, and any given security measure will provide a marginal advancement toward that goal. At this point, it is futile to look at the civil liberties side of the balance. The government side has already won.

Proponents of deference argue that if courts didn't defer, they'd be substituting their judgment for that of executive officials, who have greater expertise in understanding security issues. Special expertise in national security, however, is often not necessary for balancing security and liberty. Judges and legislators should require the experts to persuasively justify the security measures they advocate. Of course, in fields such as rocket science, nonexperts may struggle to comprehend the concepts. But security is far from rocket science.

Judges should not automatically assume that the experts always know best. Judgments made by experts can be based on unexamined customs and assumptions. The process of making experts justify their decisions is an important one, for if the experts can't convince judges that their decisions are wise, then there's a good chance that they aren't wise. A sound policy should have a sound justification.

Moreover, the deference argument conflates *evaluating* a particular security measure with *creating* such a measure. When judges review a security measure, they aren't creating their own ideal proposal but are forcing government officials to explain and justify their policies. The point of judicial review is to subject the judgment of government officials to critical scrutiny rather than to blindly accept their authority.

Whenever courts defer to the government on the effectiveness of a government security measure, they are actually deferring to the government on the ultimate question of whether the measure passes constitutional muster. This is an abdication of the well-established role of the judiciary to interpret the U.S. Constitution.

Assessing the Security Threat

In order to balance security and liberty, we must assess the security interest. This involves evaluating two components—the gravity of the security threat and the effectiveness of the security measures to address it. It is often assumed without question that the security threat from terrorism is one of the gravest dangers we face in the modern world. But this assumption might be wrong.

Assessing the risk of harm from terrorism is difficult because terrorism is such an irregular occurrence and is constantly evolving. If we examine the data from previous terrorist attacks, however, the threat of terrorism has been severely overstated. For example, many people fear being killed in a terrorist attack, but based on statistics from terrorism in the United States, the risk of dying from terrorism is minuscule. According to the political scientist John Mueller, "Even with the September 11 attacks included in the count . . . the number of Americans killed by international terrorism since the late 1960s (which is when the State Department began its accounting) is about the same as the number killed over the same period by lightning, or by accident-causing deer, or by severe allergic reactions to peanuts."[6]

Add up the eight deadliest terrorist attacks in U.S. history, and they amount to fewer than four thousand fatalities.[7] In contrast, flu and pneumonia deaths are estimated to be around sixty thousand annually. Another forty thousand die in auto accidents and other unintentional injuries each year.[8] Based on our experience with terrorism thus far, the risk of dying from terrorism is low on the relative scale of fatal risks.

Dramatic events and media attention can cloud a rational assessment of risk. The year 2001 was notable not just for the September 11 attacks. It was also the summer of the shark bite, when extensive media coverage about shark bites led to the perception that such attacks were rising dramatically. But there were fewer shark attacks in 2001 than in 2000 and fewer deaths as well: four in 2001, compared with thirteen in 2000.[9] And regardless of which year had more deaths, the number is so low that an attack is a freak occurrence.

It is true that our past experience with terrorism might not be a good indicator of the future. More treacherous terrorism is possible, such as the use of nuclear or biological weapons. This complicates our ability to assess the risk of harm from terrorism. Moreover, the intentional human conduct involved in terrorism creates a sense of outrage and fear that ordinary deaths don't engender. Alleviating fear must be taken into account, even if such fear is irrationally high in relation to other, riskier events, such as dying in a car crash. But enlightened policy must not completely give in to the irrational fear of the moment. It should attempt to quell the fear, but it must do so thoughtfully.

Nevertheless, most policymakers find it difficult to assess the threat of terrorism judiciously. In the face of widespread public panic, it is hard for government officials to make only moderate changes. Something dramatic must be done, or political heads will roll. Given the difficulty of assessing the security threat rationally, it is imperative that the courts meaningfully analyze the effectiveness of security measures. Even if panic and fear might lead to overstating the gravity of the threat, we should at least ensure that the measures taken to promote security are sufficiently effective to justify the cost.

Unfortunately, rarely do discussions about the sacrifice of civil liberties explain why security benefits can't be achieved in other ways and why such a security measure is the best and most logical one to take. Little scrutiny is given to security measures. They are often just accepted as a given, no matter how ill-conceived or ineffective they might be.

Security Theater

Some ineffective security measures, such as the New York City subway search program, are largely symbolic. The subway searches are unlikely to catch or deter terrorists because they involve only a minuscule fraction of the millions of daily passengers. Terrorists can easily turn to other targets or attempt the bombing on another day or at another train station where searches aren't taking place. The vice of symbolic security programs is that they result in needless sacrifices of liberty and drain resources from other, more effective security measures.

Nevertheless, these programs have a virtue — they can ameliorate fear because they are highly visible. Ironically, the subway search program's primary benefit was alleviating people's fear (which was probably too high), albeit in a deceptive manner (as the program did not add much in the way of security). The security expert Bruce Schneier calls such measures "security theater," for they constitute an elaborate exercise in playacting to create the appearance of security. Schneier writes:

> Security theater refers to security measures that make people feel more secure without doing anything to actually improve their security. An example: the photo ID checks that have sprung up in office buildings. No-one has ever explained why verifying that someone has a photo ID provides any actual security, but it looks like security to have a uniformed guard-for-hire looking at ID cards.[10]

Is security theater legitimate? Calming public fear is certainly a good thing, but the problem is that security theater is a lie. I believe that most people would rather know the truth than feel better through deception. Meaningful protection of rights requires that they be sacrificed only when security measures are really effective. Rights shouldn't be sacrificed for lies, no matter how noble the intention behind the lies might be.

Why No Deference Is Good for Security

Not only is a policy of no deference better for privacy rights, it is also better for security. If security officials know they'll have to justify their policies, they might be more careful about which ones they decide to use. Judicial scrutiny ensures that security officials do their jobs well and are accountable.

If we give up some privacy for security, we should at least get our money's worth, not placebos or empty symbolic measures. Judicial scrutiny demands that judges ask security officials: Are your security measures better than the alternatives? Are there other measures that invade privacy less?

We shouldn't have to just accept what others tell us and not ask questions. That isn't what rights are about. Rights are freedoms that are important enough for us to demand that courts grill the experts. In the end, the experts may be right. But when we're asked to sacrifice our rights, we should make sure the experts have thought everything through.

5

Why Privacy Isn't Merely an Individual Right

Suppose the government believes that you might be smuggling weapons. It wants to track your movements. You have an Apple iPhone, and the government can have AT&T pinpoint where you are at nearly all times (assuming the phone is turned on). A cell phone can work somewhat like a global positioning system (GPS) device. The cell phone towers must be able to locate your cell phone, and they do it through a process called "triangulation." Three cell phone towers stay connected to your phone at all times to determine precisely where you are.

On the security side of the scale, the government's interest in stopping the smuggling of weapons is very important: Dangerous unauthorized weapons can threaten all of society, and stopping them makes us all safer. On the privacy side of the scale, what gets weighed is your individual interest in the privacy of your whereabouts. So the balance is between the safety of society versus one person's privacy—and the likely outcome is that the security side will win.

In this chapter, I argue that the balance shouldn't just focus on *your* privacy—it should weigh privacy of location for everybody in society. Privacy should be understood as a societal value, not just an individual one.

Privacy as a Societal Value

"Privacy is inherently personal. The right to privacy recognizes the sovereignty of the *individual.*"[1] These are the words of one court, but they reflect the views of many in and out of the courtroom. For example, the legal scholar Thomas Emerson states that privacy "is based upon premises of individualism, that the society exists to promote the worth and the dignity of the individual. . . . The right of privacy . . . is essentially the right not to participate in the collective life — the right to shut out the community."[2]

Traditionally, rights have often been understood as protecting the individual against the incursion of society based on respect for the individual's autonomy. Many theories of privacy's value construe privacy in this manner. For example, Charles Fried argues that privacy is one of the "basic rights in persons, rights to which all are entitled equally, by virtue of their status as persons. . . . In this sense, the view is Kantian; it requires recognition of persons as ends, and forbids the overriding of their most fundamental interests for the purpose of maximizing the happiness or welfare of all."[3]

The law often sees privacy rights as individual rights. The U.S. Supreme Court has held that Fourth Amendment rights belong only to the person whom the government is searching. For example, suppose you put some things in your friend's bag. The police illegally search it and find your things. The police want to use these things to prosecute you. Does the Fourth Amendment protect you?

No. According to the Supreme Court, you can't challenge this search — even though it was improper — because it wasn't your bag.[4] The reasoning is that your rights weren't violated. The search was of your friend, and it involved rights belonging to your friend. The Supreme Court sees rights as individual possessions, and since your friend's rights don't belong to you, you're out of luck.

Communitarian scholars launch a formidable critique of traditional accounts of individual rights. The social theorist Amitai Etzioni, for example, contends that privacy is "a *societal license* that exempts a category of acts (including thoughts and emotions) from communal, public, and governmental scrutiny." For Etzioni, many theories of privacy treat it as sacrosanct, even when it conflicts with the common good. According to Etzioni, "privacy is not an absolute value and does not trump all other rights or concerns for the common good." He goes on to demonstrate how privacy interferes with greater social interests and contends that privacy often, though not always, should lose out in the balance.[5]

Etzioni is right to critique those who argue that privacy is an individual right that should trump social interests. The problem, however, is that utilitarian balancing between individual rights and the common good rarely favors individual rights — unless the interest advanced on the side of the common good is trivial. Society will generally win when its interests are balanced against those of the individual.

Etzioni, however, views individual rights as being in tension with society. The same dichotomy between individual and society that pervades liberal theories of individual rights also pervades Etzioni's communitarianism. Etzioni views the task of communitarians as "balanc[ing] individual rights with social responsibilities, and individuality with community."[6] Such a view assumes that individual and societal interests are conflicting.

In contrast, the philosopher John Dewey proposed an alternative theory about the relationship between individual and society. For Dewey, the good of individual and the good of society are often interrelated rather than antagonistic: "We cannot think of ourselves save as to some extent *social* beings. Hence we cannot separate the idea of ourselves and our own good from our idea of others and of their good."[7] Dewey contended that the value of protecting individual rights emerges from their contribution to society. In other words, individual rights are not trumps but are protections by society from its intrusiveness. Society makes space for the individual because of the social benefits this space provides. Therefore, Dewey argues, rights should be valued based on "the contribution they make to the welfare of the community." Otherwise, in any kind of utilitarian calculus, individual rights wouldn't be valuable enough to outweigh most social interests, and it would be impossible to justify individual rights. Dewey argued that we must insist upon a "social basis and social justification" for civil liberties.[8]

Like Dewey, I contend the value of protecting the individual is a social one. Society involves a great deal of friction, and we are constantly clashing with one another. Part of what makes a society a good place in which to live is the extent to which it allows people freedom from the intrusiveness of others. A society without privacy protection would be oppressive. When protecting individual rights, we as a society decide to hold back in order to receive the benefits of creating free zones for individuals to flourish.

As the legal theorist Robert Post has argued, privacy is not merely a set of restraints on society's rules and norms. Instead, privacy constitutes a society's attempt to promote civility.[9] Society protects privacy as a means of enforcing order in the community. Privacy isn't the trumpeting of the individual against society's interests but the protection of the individual based on society's own norms and values. Privacy isn't simply a way to extricate individuals from social control; it is itself a form of social control that emerges from a society's norms. It is not an external restraint on society but an internal dimension of society. Therefore, privacy has a social value. When the law protects the individual, it does so not just for the individual's sake but for the sake of society. Privacy thus shouldn't be weighed as an individual right against the greater social good. Privacy issues involve balancing societal interests on both sides of the scale.[10]

Surveillance of Movement

Let's return to the issue I began the chapter with—the government wants to track your location. Although you're the one raising the court challenge against the surveillance, the court shouldn't focus its balance just on protecting you. At stake in the case are not just your rights but everybody's rights to the privacy of their movement.

If the court focuses merely on your individual rights, the balance becomes skewed. Suppose you really are guilty of smuggling weapons. On one side of the scale is your ability to exercise your right to privacy in order to carry out a crime. On the other side is society's interest in maintaining safety and order. Society clearly wins if the balance is understood in this way.

Even if you're innocent, the balance is hard for you to win. Stopping the smuggling might save countless lives. So what if your privacy is violated? If the government made a mistake and tracked your movements when you were innocent, it will soon realize its error. The government could send you an apology note, saying:

> We're sorry we violated your privacy. But we had a really important need to investigate the smuggling of weapons. Stopping this crime can save many lives. Once we discovered you were innocent, we ceased our surveillance of you. We realize you might have been harmed by this, but think of how much good your sacrifice did for society. Sometimes you have to take one for the team. Thank you.

Fondly,

The Government
Keeping you safe and secure, since 1789

The problem with this argument is that you're not the only one harmed by this practice. The power of the government to engage in this kind of surveillance without adequate oversight affects everyone. It shapes the kind of society we live in. Moreover, the government can engage in systemic surveillance that dramatically increases its power and has widespread effects on people's freedom.

Many of the most important Supreme Court cases were brought by some rather unsavory criminals. They might have done some awful things, and they might not be heroes, but they are champions of the law. Many of them probably fought only for their own selfish interests. If asked why they were fighting, many might have said: "I'm fighting for *my* rights!" But their cases affected us all, and shaped the meaning of our Constitution. They didn't just fight for their rights. They fought for the rights of all of us.

PART II

Times of Crisis

How the Law Should Address Matters of

National Security

The Pendulum Argument

6

A common argument is that in times of crisis, we must sacrifice civil liberties to gain security. Judge Richard Posner contends that the "events of September 11 revealed the United States to be in greater jeopardy from international terrorism than had been believed by most people until then. . . . It stands to reason that such a revelation would lead to our civil liberties being curtailed."[1] The Constitution is not a "suicide pact," Posner observes, using the words of U.S. Supreme Court Justice Robert Jackson.[2] Constitutional rights must be limited in times of crisis. This process is inevitable, Posner asserts, and we should accept it without being unduly concerned because rights are often restored during times of peace. We should not treat "our existing civil liberties—protections of privacy, of the freedom of the press, of the rights of criminal suspects, and the rest—as sacrosanct and insist[] therefore that the battle against international terrorism must accommodate itself to them."[3]

Likewise, William Rehnquist, the late chief justice of the U.S. Supreme Court, observed: "It is neither desirable nor is it remotely likely that civil liberty will occupy as favored a position in wartime as it does in peacetime."[4] The sociologist Amitai Etzioni contends that the curtailment of rights during times of crisis doesn't threaten constitutional democracy. Instead, it represents a democracy's responsiveness to public fears. "Once safety is restored," he states, "the [security] measures can gradually be rolled back."[5]

I refer to this argument as the "pendulum argument"—during times of crisis, the pendulum swings toward security and rights are curtailed, and during times of peace, the pendulum swings back toward liberty, and rights are restored. But the pendulum argument has it exactly backward—times of crisis are *precisely* when we should be at our staunchest in protecting privacy and liberty.

Unnecessary Sacrifices

The pendulum argument begins with the assumption that sacrifices of rights and civil liberties are necessary in times of crisis, a view many share. One poll shortly after the September 11th attacks asked: "Would you be willing to give up some of the liberties we have in this country in order for the government to crack down on terrorism, or not?" About 68 percent of respondents said yes.[6] In another poll in early 2002, about 78 percent declared themselves "more willing to give up certain freedoms to improve safety and security."[7]

In response to increased security measures to combat terrorism, countless people say: "I'd gladly give away some of my privacy if I can be kept secure." The argument treats the sacrifice as a temporary response to a dire situation. For example, even the celebrated constitutional rights lawyer Floyd Abrams has argued that "we must accept that we now live at a level of vulnerability which requires distressing steps of a continuing nature in an effort to protect ourselves. As a result, we must, I think, be prepared to yield some of our privacy, to accept a higher level of surveillance of our conduct, even to risk some level of confrontation with the Fourth Amendment of the United States Constitution."[8]

But in many circumstances the assumption that rights and civil liberties must be sacrificed for security is invalid. During times of crisis, the government—often with the support of a majority of the public—is far too willing to make unnecessary sacrifices. These sacrifices often involve the rights and liberties of minorities and dissidents, so the costs aren't borne equally by all in society. When people say they're willing to give up rights and liberties in the name of security, they're often sacrificing the rights and liberties of others rather than their own.

Why We Readily Sacrifice Billy Budd

Herman Melville's classic novella *Billy Budd*, written late in the nineteenth century, bears an uncanny relevance to our times. *Billy Budd* is a moving depiction of a profound sacrifice made in the name of security.[9] Billy Budd, a kindhearted and simple sailor, is falsely accused of mutiny by an officer of the ship who acts out of personal animus toward Billy. Billy speaks with a stutter, and can't speak at all when under stress. In frustration, his arm shoots out almost reflexively, and he hits the officer so hard that he kills him.

The ship's captain, Edward Vere, convenes a secret military tribunal.[10] Billy's adjudicators all believe that his life should be spared because the killing was unintentional. However, the governing law, the Articles of War, appears to be strict and uncompromising—Billy caused the officer's death, and therefore he must be condemned. At the trial, Vere delivers an eloquent speech to the adjudicators explaining that no matter how great the temptation to be more merciful, the law is strict and controlling, and the rule of law must be followed. This is especially true, Vere argues, during times of war, when maintaining discipline and order is imperative. Billy is convicted and is executed by hanging the next day.

Commentators have often viewed Vere as caught up in a difficult situation, forced to choose between adhering to the rule of law or adopting a more equitable approach that would obviate the sacrifice of Billy Budd. Vere chooses to follow the law's unbending strictures . . . or so he would have us believe. A lot of evidence in the novel suggests that Vere actively manipulates the law in order to hang Billy Budd.[11] In particular, Vere doesn't follow the proper procedure and wait for his ship to rejoin the squadron, where Billy could be tried in a more flexible manner. More lenient sanctions are available at tribunals held with the full squadron. Instead, Vere rushes to convene a makeshift trial on board his ship while it is alone at sea.

Although pretending to be governed by the strict rule of law, Vere really uses the law as a tool to sacrifice Billy Budd. He does so because he fears a mutiny. Vere makes a persuasive argument to officers deciding Billy's fate, urging them to convict Billy because failing to do so would make the ship's commanders look cowardly. Billy Budd must be sacrificed not because he poses a threat, but because sparing his life might appear as a sign of weakness to the crew. Throughout the novella, Melville provides subtle clues that Vere acts out of his own insecurity rather than exercising sound judgment.

The Lessons of History

Like Captain Vere, our government often makes profound sacrifices during times of crisis. Throughout U.S. history, significant curtailments of rights have been carried out in the name of national security and wartime necessity. During the Civil War, President Lincoln suspended habeas corpus. During World War I, individuals who spoke out against the war were prosecuted. During World War II, the government rounded up around 120,000 people of Japanese descent living on the West Coast and imprisoned them in internment camps.[12] During the Cold War, hundreds of people were subjected to interrogation and blacklisting for their communist beliefs.

The law has often failed to stop government officials from making these painful sacrifices. For example, during World War I, the

U.S. Supreme Court upheld the convictions of people who were speaking out against the war. "When a nation is at war," the Supreme Court declared, "many things that might be said in time of peace are such a hindrance to its effort that their utterance will not be endured so long as men fight and that no Court could regard them as protected by any constitutional right."[13] The Supreme Court also upheld the Japanese internment, concluding that "the military authorities considered that the need for action was great, and time was short. We cannot—by availing ourselves of the calm perspective of hindsight—now say that at that time these actions were unjustified."[14] As the Court explained,

> In a case of threatened danger requiring prompt action, it is a choice between inflicting obviously needless hardship on the many, or sitting passive and unresisting in the presence of the threat. We think that constitutional government, in time of war, is not so powerless and does not compel so hard a choice if those charged with the responsibility of our national defense have reasonable ground for believing that the threat is real.[15]

When these curtailments were later reexamined, they turned out to be unnecessary overreactions. The Japanese internment has long been acknowledged to have been a terrible mistake, and the U.S. government has formally apologized.[16] The Supreme Court is much more protective of antiwar speech today than it was during World War I. The McCarthy-era fear of Communists has widely been acknowledged to have been a significant overreaction.[17] Recently released evidence suggests that McCarthy may have deliberately misled the public about the threat posed by Communists in the United States.[18] In short, during times of crisis, our leaders have made profound sacrifices in the name of security, ones that we later realized need not have been made.

But history has repeated itself. After September 11, the government made a series of significant curtailments of privacy and civil liberties.

For example, it secretly rounded up and detained thousands of "enemy combatants" living in the United States and refused to reveal their identities.[19] It interned them indefinitely in camps, denying them hearings, representation by counsel, and even contact with the outside world.[20]

The courts reacted quite similarly to the way they had acted before. In *Hamdi v. Rumsfeld*, the Supreme Court held that it was within the president's power to detain Yassar Hamdi, an American citizen captured during military operations in Afghanistan, as an "enemy combatant." The Court concluded that executive power is limited by the due-process clause, which requires that enemy combatants be afforded some degree of individual process. However, the Court stated that the amount of process accorded is not akin to that regularly provided. Although people detained as enemy combatants are protected by some "core rights," the Court noted that "the full protections that accompany challenges to detentions in other settings may prove unworkable and inappropriate in the enemy-combatant setting."[21]

Were the curtailments in liberty necessary? The debate goes on, but it has been acknowledged that even if some of the government's actions were useful, they were excessive. In 2003 the inspector general of the Department of Justice reported that the government overreacted after September 11 and improperly rounded up numerous individuals.[22] In 2004 the U.S. government abruptly released Hamdi after holding him for almost three years in solitary confinement without any criminal charges, stating that he was no longer a threat.[23]

Rejecting the Sacrifices

It is far too easy to succumb to Vere's beguiling argument to sacrifice Billy Budd for the sake of security. We should be suspicious of these arguments. We must give the highest scrutiny to the sacrifices our leaders make in the name of security.

Judge Posner contends that to the extent that the government has overreacted by curtailing liberty in times of crisis, we shouldn't be concerned, since the "curtailment of civil liberties in the Civil War, World War I (and the ensuing 'Red Scare'), World War II, and the Cold War did not outlast the emergencies."[24] But curtailments of liberties harmed thousands of innocent citizens, sometimes quite severely. The Japanese internment deprived countless people of their freedom. The McCarthy-era hunt for Communists during the 1950s resulted in many people being fired from their jobs and blacklisted from employment for years.[25]

We shouldn't simply accept these mistakes as inevitable; we should seek to prevent them from occurring. Hoping that the pendulum will swing back offers little consolation to those whose liberties are infringed. The government's eventual realization that it overreacted and its issuing an apology doesn't set everything right. Apologies aren't meaningful if one continues to make the same mistakes.

Of course, not all sacrifices are unwarranted. Sometimes sacrifices in rights and civil liberties should be made, but only when the government adequately justifies why they are necessary. We must subject proposed sacrifices to meticulous scrutiny since it is easy for judgments in times of crisis to be skewed by fear. In light of a history marred by frequent misguided responses to threats, we should be extra cautious about making needless sacrifices.

Not only is the pendulum argument wrong in falsely assuming that sacrifices of rights and civil liberties are necessary, it also misses the point about why rights and civil liberties matter. The protection of liberty is most important in times of crisis, when it is under the greatest threat. During times of peace, because we are less likely to make unnecessary sacrifices of liberty, the need to protect it is not as dire. The greatest need for safeguarding liberty comes during times when we least want to protect it, when our fear clouds our judgment. We most need rights when the going gets tough—to stop us and make us think before we let our leaders hang Billy Budd.

7

The National-Security Argument

Many people argue that the government should be regulated much less when it pursues matters of national security than when it investigates ordinary crime. They contend that national-security threats are quite different from the dangers of crime. For example, as Andrew McCarthy, senior fellow of the Foundation for the Defense of Democracies and former federal prosecutor, testified to Congress:

> We want constitutional rights to protect Americans from oppressive executive action. We do not, however, want constitutional rights to be converted by enemies of the United States into weapons in their war against us. We want courts to be a vigorous check against overbearing governmental tactics in the investigation and prosecution of Americans for ordinary violations of law; but we do not—or, at least, we should not—want courts to degrade the effectiveness of executive action targeted at enemies of the United States who seek to kill Americans and undermine their liberties.[1]

Those who maintain the exceptionalism of national-security threats propose weaker Fourth Amendment requirements or none at all. They contend that matters involving national security must be kept secret and should be insulated from close scrutiny. Should matters of national security be given special treatment? In this chapter, I argue that the distinction between matters of national security and regular crime is too fuzzy and incoherent to be workable.

The Law of National Security

In 1969 the three founding members of a group called "the White Panthers" bombed a CIA office in Michigan. The group wasn't a white supremacist group; in fact, they supported the goals of the Black Panther Party. They also advocated radical anarchist goals, arguing that everything should be free and that money should be abolished. The group's manifesto stated: "We demand total freedom for everybody! And we will not be stopped until we get it. . . . ROCK AND ROLL music is the spearhead of our attack because it is so effective and so much fun."[2]

During its investigation of the crime, the government wiretapped calls made by one of the bombers. The wiretapping was conducted without warrants supported by probable cause required by the Fourth Amendment.

The case made its way up to the U.S. Supreme Court in 1972. The Nixon administration argued that because the bombing involved a threat to national security, the government wasn't bound by the Fourth Amendment. The administration argued the U.S. Constitution grants the president special national-security powers to "preserve, protect and defend the Constitution of the United States," and these powers trump the regular protections of the Fourth Amendment.[3]

The Supreme Court rebuffed President Nixon's claim that he could ignore Fourth Amendment rights in the name of national security:

> [W]e do not think a case has been made for the requested departure from Fourth Amendment standards. The circumstances

described do not justify complete exemption of domestic security surveillance from prior judicial scrutiny. Official surveillance, whether its purpose be criminal investigation or ongoing intelligence gathering, risks infringement of constitutionally protected privacy of speech. Security surveillances are especially sensitive because of the inherent vagueness of the domestic security concept, the necessarily broad and continuing nature of intelligence gathering, and the temptation to utilize such surveillances to oversee political dissent. We recognize, as we have before, the constitutional basis of the President's domestic security role, but we think it must be exercised in a manner compatible with the Fourth Amendment. In this case we hold that this requires an appropriate prior warrant procedure.[4]

The Court noted that the Fourth Amendment might require slightly different procedures for matters of national security depending upon practical considerations.[5] Thus Fourth Amendment regulation is flexible to the particular needs of the situation.

Despite the Supreme Court's rejection of the argument that national security should entail a dramatic departure from constitutional protections, the national-security argument is still invoked. The legal scholar Stephen Vladeck notes that the concept of national security has a distorting effect on the law: "[O]ne can find national security considerations influencing ordinary judicial decision making across the entire gamut of contemporary civil and criminal litigation."[6] Although claims of national security don't directly eliminate rights or civil liberties, they severely weaken them. National-security claims are often accompanied by calls for deference (which, as I argued in Chapter 4, are unjustified), as well as demands for secrecy.

What Precisely Is "National Security"?

In 1999 two high school students, Eric Harris and Dylan Klebold, went on a rampage at the Columbine High School near Denver.

They killed thirteen people, injured twenty-one others, and then committed suicide. The crime, though, wasn't categorized as a national-security matter even though it involved guns, terror, mass murder, bombs, and suicidal perpetrators.

In contrast, in 2002, the government suspected José Padilla of plotting to detonate a "dirty bomb" (a bomb with radioactive material) in a major city. He was designated an "enemy combatant" and detained and tortured for years without being charged with a crime or accorded the right to a hearing. Ultimately, the dirty-bomb allegations were dropped, and he was convicted of conspiracy to provide material support to terrorists and sentenced to seventeen years in prison.[7] Padilla was a U.S. citizen. Why was his crime deemed a national-security issue while the Columbine rampage wasn't?

The line between national-security and regular criminal activities is quite blurry. What about the Beltway snipers of 2002, who terrorized people in Maryland, Virginia, and the District of Columbia? What about Timothy McVeigh, the man who bombed the Alfred P. Murrah Federal Building in Oklahoma City, killing 168 people? Are these regular crimes? Or matters of national security? Is there a meaningful difference?

How should national-security threats be distinguished from other crimes? One way is to focus on the number of potential victims, with matters of national security involving a larger number of casualties than ordinary crime. Under this approach, however, a serial killer might be deemed a national-security threat but not an assassin who attempts to murder the president. How many victims does it take to turn an ordinary crime into a national-security issue? Unfortunately, there's no simple answer.

Another way to distinguish between the two classes of crime is to focus on the means of attack. Perhaps if bombs are involved, then it's a national-security issue. But bomb threats occur all the time in buildings across the country. Many turn out to be hoaxes by disgruntled employees. Are these national-security issues? Recently, a man flew a plane into an IRS building because he objected to income tax.[8] Is this a national-security issue since it involved crashing a plane into a government building? The problem with using means of attack as a way to distinguish national-security issues from ordinary crime is that any means of attack can be used by terrorists as well as by ordinary criminals.

It is difficult to distinguish national-security matters from ordinary crime, especially when U.S. citizens are involved. National-security threats *are* a form of crime. They are severe crimes, but the rules for investigating ordinary crime are designed to regulate government information gathering no matter how grave the particular crime might be. These rules aren't rigid, and they make allowances for exigencies and unusual circumstances.

Improper Invocations of "National Security"

"National security" has often been abused as a justification not only for surveillance but also for maintaining the secrecy of government records as well as for violating the civil liberties of citizens. The Japanese internment during World War II, as well as many other abuses, was authorized in the name of national security. As the court noted in *United States v. Ehrlichman*, the Watergate burglary was an example of the misuse of national-security powers: "The danger of leaving delicate decisions of propriety and probable cause to those actually assigned to ferret out 'national security' information is potent, and is indeed illustrated by the intrusion undertaken in this case."[9]

The government has often raised national-security concerns to conceal embarrassing and scandalous documents from the public — documents which often turned out to be harmless, such as the Pentagon Papers, a study of the U.S. military and political involvement in Vietnam.[10] Daniel Ellsberg, an analyst who worked on the study, gave the Pentagon Papers to the *New York Times*. The government sought to prevent publication by claiming that disclosing the Pentagon Papers would create a "grave and immediate danger to the security of the United States."[11] But this claim was false. The U.S. Supreme Court rejected the government's attempt to stop the Pentagon Papers from being disclosed, and national security wasn't harmed after they were published. Solicitor General Edwin Griswold, who wrote the government's brief, later recanted, stating that he hadn't seen "any trace of a threat to national security" in the Pentagon Papers.[12] The dire claims the government made about national security were bogus, just a way to cover up what the Pentagon Papers revealed—that the government had made deceptive claims about the Vietnam War.

After the September 11 attacks, the government began using a tactic called the "state secrets privilege" to exclude evidence in a case if it will reveal a classified secret.[13] Even if the government isn't a party to the case, it can swoop in and invoke the privilege. Many times, the case gets dismissed because a person can't prove her case without the evidence. Tom Blanton, director of George Washington University's National Security Archive, says that the state secrets privilege acts like a "neutron bomb" on a case, effectively wiping it out.[14]

For example, in one case, a German citizen named Khaled El-Masri sued the CIA, claiming that he had been kidnapped by CIA agents in Europe, taken to a secret prison in Afghanistan, and tortured—a procedure called "rendition." Khaled said he was "beaten, drugged, bound, and blindfolded during transport; confined in a small, unsanitary cell; interrogated several times; and consistently prevented from communicating with anyone outside the detention facility, including his family." According to news accounts, he "was made to drink water so putrid it made him vomit," and he "slept on a single blanket, shivered through the cold months and was fed chicken bones and skin." After five months, the CIA finally realized it had the wrong man, and Khaled was released. An unidentified CIA officer was quoted in a news article saying that the CIA "picked up the wrong people, who had no information. In many, many cases there was only some vague association [with terrorism]."[15]

Khaled sued the CIA because, as he explained, he wanted the Agency "to admit that injustice was done. I'd like an explanation and I'd like an apology." The government asserted the state secrets privilege and demanded that the case be immediately dismissed. The U.S. Court of Appeals for the Fourth Circuit agreed. The court reasoned that in order for the government to defend itself against Khaled's allegations, it would have to disclose details about how it interrogated him, and that would reveal state secrets.[16]

It is hard to believe there wasn't a way to protect sensitive information while allowing the case to go forward. Khaled argued that a lot of details about the case had been widely reported by the media, but the court concluded that allowing the case to proceed would also expose "how the CIA organizes, staffs, and supervises its most sensitive intelligence operations." Khaled contended that perhaps the evidence could have been revealed only to his attorney and the judge, with his attorney obtaining a security clearance. But the court concluded that even the judge alone couldn't see the evidence.[17]

Why shouldn't Khaled's allegations be vetted? If the CIA was engaging in illegal torture and interrogation tactics, its actions should be subject to some kind of review. The state secrets privilege effectively immunizes the CIA from any challenge to its activities, even if those activities are illegal.

Ironically, the case that gave rise to the state secrets privilege involved an improper use of secrecy. In *United States v. Reynolds*, a U.S. Air Force plane exploded in flight, killing nine people. Only four people were able to parachute to safety. The widows of three civilians who died in the accident sued the government for negligence. In a civil lawsuit, plaintiffs are ordinarily entitled to see documents pertaining to an accident, and the plaintiffs in this case wanted to see the

Air Force's accident report and other evidence surrounding the incident. But the government withheld these documents due to national-security concerns. The government wouldn't even allow the trial judge to examine the documents to evaluate the government's claim that their disclosure would undermine national security.

The U.S. Supreme Court upheld the government's actions under the state secrets privilege, declaring that "when the formal claim of privilege was filed by the Secretary of the Air Force, under circumstances indicating a reasonable possibility that military secrets were involved, there was certainly a sufficient showing of privilege to cut off further demand for the document."[18] The Court deferred to the government's assertions; indeed, it even refused to examine the accident report. When the report was eventually declassified forty-seven years later, it revealed no state secrets. Instead, it showed that the government had been negligent. In his book about the case, Louis Fisher, a senior scholar at the Library of Congress, concludes that the government "falsely described" the documents and "misled" the courts.[19]

Certainly, there are times where the government has a compelling reason to keep information secret. But it is currently far too easy for the government to cry "national security" to conceal unseemly information. Claims of secrecy in the name of national security must be subjected to rigorous scrutiny.

Keeping Claims of "National Security" under Control

Although the president has extensive powers to protect the country, these powers must be carefully circumscribed so as not allow the president to circumvent constitutional rights and other legal protections. National security is a nebulous concept that too often is used to justify decreased regulation, oversight, and accountability.

At a minimum, claims of national security should be examined with great skepticism. Every decade—perhaps in every census year—Congress should thoroughly investigate government activities in the name of national security as well as government demands for secrecy. Such a project was undertaken by Congress in 1975. when the Church Committee reported on government surveillance activities and abuses. This endeavor led to many reforms and legal protections—it was one of the inspirations for the creation of the Foreign Intelligence Surveillance Act (FISA). Reviews such as the one done by the Church Committee should be carried out regularly and more frequently. Such reviews will bring needed transparency and accountability to government activities in the name of national security.[20]

8

The Problem with Dissolving the Crime-Espionage Distinction

For a long time, the law has maintained separate rules to regulate investigation of ordinary crime and espionage, the gathering of foreign intelligence. The rules regulating criminal investigations are generally much stricter than those regulating espionage.

This division—which I call the "crime-espionage distinction"—is sensible because gathering intelligence is different from investigating or preventing a crime. The rules governing espionage are permissive, allowing the government broad surveillance power and a lot of secrecy. The rules regulating criminal investigations are more rigorous and have more transparency, ensuring that the government doesn't infringe upon people's rights and civil liberties.

After September 11, however, many proponents of heightened security argued that terrorism investigations should be regulated by the rules for espionage rather than the rules for criminal investigations. In terrorism cases the government gathers information to investigate criminal activity as well as to acquire foreign intelligence. It is difficult to classify terrorism investigations as purely about crime or purely about espionage. Many government officials, politicians, and commentators argued that maintaining the crime-espionage distinction in terrorism cases prevented useful sharing of information among government agencies. These arguments prevailed, resulting in changes in the law that significantly eroded the crime-espionage distinction.

In this chapter, I argue that the crime-espionage distinction should have been kept intact. The crime-espionage distinction establishes a careful balance between two very different government functions—criminal investigation and espionage. The rules governing espionage are inadequate for protecting rights and civil liberties, as they are designed to regulate the clandestine world of spying. Dissolving the distinction allows the weak rules governing espionage to replace stricter rules that used to govern in many areas.

Two Systems of Regulation

The Fourth Amendment

The Fourth Amendment mandates strong judicial oversight and regulation when the government gathers information about people. It typically requires that the government justify its belief that searches or surveillance will turn up evidence of a crime. The U.S. Supreme Court has suggested that espionage is a special category of surveillance that might not be regulated by the Fourth Amendment, but it has never resolved the matter.[1]

Espionage is indeed quite different from criminal investigations, and it is sensible that the two should be regulated differently. Requiring the government to justify how its information gathering will reveal evidence of a crime is inimical to foreign intelligence gathering, where the government's goal is to learn about the activities of foreign agents regardless of whether criminal activity is involved. For example, the Soviet embassy in Washington, D.C., was long the source of a spy-versus-spy game during the Cold War. The U.S. intelligence agencies made countless attempts to eavesdrop on embassy activities, spying on it from a nearby house and even digging a secret tunnel beneath it. Much of this surveillance didn't relate to any criminal investigation—it involved spying and counterspying.

Federal Statutory Law

Federal statutory law has long recognized the crime-espionage distinction. Electronic surveillance to investigate crime is regulated by a federal law called the Electronic Communications Privacy Act (ECPA), which provides strong protections of privacy. It requires government officials to justify their belief that the surveillance will uncover evidence of a crime. It requires government officials to explain to the court why alternative investigative methods won't be effective. When issuing orders allowing electronic surveillance, courts will mandate that law-enforcement officials minimize listening in when innocent people are involved.

A separate statute regulates espionage. Passed in 1978, the Foreign Intelligence Surveillance Act (FISA) establishes procedures for government officials to gather foreign intelligence within U.S. borders.[2] FISA is permissive, affording the government much more expansive surveillance power than it would have for criminal investigations under ECPA. FISA permits electronic surveillance and covert searches pursuant to court orders, which are reviewed by a special court of eleven federal judges known as the Foreign Intelligence Surveillance Court (FISC). The court meets in secret, with the government presenting applications for orders. If the government receives an adverse decision, it can appeal to a three-judge panel.

FISA's regulations are much looser than those for ordinary crime. For ordinary crime, surveillance is authorized only if there is a showing of probable cause that the surveillance will uncover evidence of criminal activity. Under FISA, orders are granted if there is probable cause to believe that the monitored party is a "foreign power" or "an agent of a foreign power."[3] FISA surveillance is therefore not tied to any required suspicion of wrongdoing. FISA orders are much broader than those under ECPA, allowing for more surveillance and less judicial oversight. For example, an order under FISA can authorize electronic surveillance for three to four times as long as an order under ECPA. People subjected to surveillance under ECPA are always informed about it at some point. Under FISA, the surveillance can be kept secret indefinitely, potentially forever. And even in a trial, ECPA allows defendants to examine the documents justifying the surveillance, but FISA doesn't.[4]

The FISA "Wall"

For a long time, the ECPA and FISA regimes were kept separate by strict limits on FISA's scope. For example, suppose a government official was investigating a crime and wanted to use the more lenient provisions of FISA to gather information about a suspect. FISA required that the primary purpose of the investigation be foreign intelligence gathering. Because the official was really interested in investigating a crime, he wouldn't have been allowed to use FISA and would have had to follow ECPA's rules instead.

The two realms weren't completely separate. If intelligence officials learned about a crime while gathering intelligence under FISA, they were allowed to share the evidence with criminal investigators. For example, in one case, the FBI was spying on Zein Hassan Isa and his wife, Maria Matias, who lived in Missouri.[5] Although Isa was a naturalized citizen, the FBI suspected he was an agent of the Palestine Liberation Organization (PLO). The FBI obtained an order under FISA to bug Isa's home. Recall that a FISA order doesn't have the same protections as an order under ECPA. If the FBI were investigating Isa for a crime, it would need to go through the more stringent procedures of ECPA and the Fourth Amendment. But the FBI wasn't looking for crime—it was gathering foreign intelligence.

One evening, the FBI's bugs recorded a loud shouting match between Zein, Maria, and their sixteen-year old daughter, Tina. The parents were furious because of Tina's rebelliousness and the fact she was dating someone. Suddenly, Zein declared: "Here, listen, my dear daughter, do you know that this is the last day? Tonight, you're going to die!"

"Huh?" Tina responded. Maria held Tina down, and Zein approached her with a knife. Zein stabbed her repeatedly in the chest, declaring, "Quiet, little one! Die my daughter, die!" The FBI turned the recording over to the state police, and these tapes were used to convict the Isas of murder. They were sentenced to death.[6]

The Isas argued that the court shouldn't have allowed the recording at trial since it was obtained under the looser regulation of FISA. But the court disagreed. Because investigating a crime wasn't the purpose of the FBI's investigation, it wasn't abusing FISA. The FBI happened to discover evidence of a crime, and there was no sensible reason not to use it.[7]

There are times, however, when the government engages in foreign intelligence gathering and criminal investigation simultaneously. This often happens with terrorism investigations. What should the government do under these circumstances? Before the scope of FISA was expanded, the government would use a so-called wall. Those investigating the crime would be walled off from those conducting the surveillance. This procedure would prevent the criminal investigators from telling intelligence officials to do their bidding, an obvious end-run around the crime-espionage distinction and Fourth Amendment protections. Those doing the surveillance could always pass along evidence of any crimes they might find—as was done in the Isa case. The key was that the criminal investigators didn't take charge of the surveillance.

Dissolving the Crime-Espionage Distinction

After the September 11 attacks, many proponents of increased security blamed the FISA wall for the failure of agencies to share information they had prior to 9/11. For example, Paul Rosenzweig, a fellow of the Heritage Foundation, argued that "the artificial limitations" of the FISA wall were "a relic of a bygone era" and incompatible with dealing with the threat of terrorism.[8] John Yoo, who was one of the architects of the Bush administration's antiterrorism policies, noted that the wall "played a role in our failure to stop the 9/11 attacks" by impeding information sharing.[9] Critics of the wall pointed to the fact that during the summer before the September 11 attacks, the FBI and CIA had been observing some of the terrorists. In some instances, FBI agents had refused to share information with other agents because they believed the FISA wall would not allow it.[10]

The Bush administration successfully pushed Congress to expand FISA and eliminate the wall. Before the expansion of FISA's scope, the rules regulating espionage applied only when "the purpose" of the investigation was to gather foreign intelligence. The Patriot Act enlarged FISA's scope to apply when foreign intelligence gathering was "a significant purpose" of the investigation.[11]

This seemingly subtle change has dramatic ramifications. With the change in language from "*the* purpose" to "*a significant* purpose," foreign intelligence gathering no longer needs to be the primary purpose of the surveillance. The government can now rely on loose FISA protections even when foreign intelligence gathering is only one of many goals. After this change in the law, Attorney General John Ashcroft virtually eliminated the FISA wall. The government now needs only to articulate one purpose of the investigation that doesn't involve gathering evidence for criminal prosecution.[12]

This is a troubling development because government investigations of alleged terrorist activities often have a large scope and multiple purposes. Since FISA surveillance information can be used in criminal trials, it increasingly can become a tool for law enforcement and an end-run around the protections of ECPA. Maintaining the crime-espionage distinction is important because FISA's looser rules aren't adequate to regulate criminal investigations. FISA deals with intelligence gathering, where the goal is to collect information broadly. FISA's rules are designed with this purpose in mind. On the other hand, ECPA's rules are designed to protect privacy by forcing government officials to justify the need for surveillance by demonstrating suspicion of criminal activity. In other words, under ECPA, you need to be suspected of wrongdoing for the government to be able to put you under surveillance. But under FISA, you can be totally innocent, since the goal is general information gathering.

Compounding this problem is FISA's secrecy. Under FISA, the entire proceedings are held in secret between the government and the court. Nobody is present to argue the opposing side.[13] As the national-security law experts William Banks and M. E. Bowman observe, the "secrecy that attends FISC proceedings, and the limitations imposed on judicial review of FISA surveillance, may insulate unconstitutional surveillance from any effective sanction."[14] FISA's high level of secrecy is appropriate for matters of espionage but not for matters of law enforcement in general. Unlimited secrecy eliminates accountability and prevents the public from being able to understand and evaluate the government's actions, especially when they affect people's rights and civil liberties.

Thus the realms of ECPA (criminal investigation) and FISA (espionage) must be kept distinct because FISA's sweeping surveillance powers would undermine the primary way of keeping law-enforcement investigations limited and in check. Espionage is governed by rules that enable sweeping and secret surveillance without any suspicion of lawbreaking. These rules must not become the norm for criminal investigations, for they clash with the way the Fourth

Amendment protects privacy and civil liberties—by constraining government information gathering, mandating public accountability, and requiring suspicion of wrongdoing.

The FBI, which handles domestic criminal activities, and the CIA, which engages in spying, were created as separate agencies for a reason. Nazi Germany's Gestapo, the Soviet Union's KGB, and the police-intelligence systems of other totalitarian countries blended these functions. When creating the CIA, President Truman declared that "this country wanted no Gestapo under any guise or for any reason."[15] The crime-espionage distinction prevents the kind of broad spying on citizens performed by the Gestapo.

The Case of Brandon Mayfield

Consider the case of Brandon Mayfield.[16] In 2004 a terrorist bombing on trains in Madrid killed 191 people. Spanish police found fingerprints at the scene on a plastic bag with explosive detonators inside. The FBI assisted in the investigation by searching its extensive database of fingerprints, and it found a few potential matches. One of those matches was Brandon Mayfield. Mayfield was a U.S. citizen residing with his wife and three children near Portland, Oregon. A retired army officer, he practiced law for a living. He was a Muslim, having converted after he met his wife, who was Egyptian. At the time of the investigation, he was thirty-eight years old.

The FBI thought Mayfield's fingerprints were a match, and they began to watch him and his family in public. To further investigate Mayfield and his family, the FBI sought an order under FISA to enter and search Mayfield's home and to engage in electronic surveillance. The order was granted. The FBI bugged Mayfield's home, covertly searched it, and wiretapped his office and home phones. When the FBI accidentally left behind traces of its search of Mayfield's house while the family was away, Mayfield thought he had been burglarized. The incident frightened his family.

Mayfield was arrested and jailed, during which time his family couldn't visit him. The FBI relayed Mayfield's fingerprints to the Spanish police. The Spanish police, however, disagreed that the fingerprints matched, finding many differences between Mayfield's prints and the ones on the bag. Eventually, the Spanish authorities matched the fingerprint to an Algerian man.

The FBI released Mayfield and apologized to him and his family. The Mayfields sued the government, which settled with them for $2 million and agreed to destroy the information it had obtained through FISA.

Should Mayfield have been investigated under FISA? He was a U.S. citizen. The focus of the investigation was clearly criminal. He hadn't traveled abroad in ten years and had never before been arrested. Nevertheless, the government used the loose rules for foreign intelligence gathering rather than the stricter rules for criminal investigations.

Thus Mayfield wasn't afforded the normal protections a U.S. citizen is guaranteed when the government suspects him of a crime. The case illustrates how blurring the distinction between criminal investigation and espionage can diminish the oversight and regulation of law-enforcement officials and threaten people's rights and civil liberties.

Why the Distinction Should Be Restored

FISA's scope shouldn't have been expanded. The *9/11 Commission Report* concluded that the government officials who didn't share information were "confused about the rules governing the sharing and use of information gathered in intelligence channels."[17] In other words, the problem wasn't that the FISA wall was too restrictive.

The problem was that the government officials didn't understand it well enough. The proper response should have been to better educate the agents, not to enlarge FISA's domain and dismantle the wall.

But David Kris, a former associate deputy attorney general in the U.S. Department of Justice, defends the dismantling of the wall. He argues that law-enforcement officials can be of great help in foreign intelligence gathering because they have expertise and powers that intelligence officials may lack.[18] This is true, but the active participation of law enforcement when U.S. citizens are involved dissolves the crime-espionage distinction. This distinction is essential to prevent government espionage from swamping the system we have in place to protect privacy rights and civil liberties. The government shouldn't be allowed to use its greater powers of espionage as a substitute for the more regulated and controlled powers it has for investigating crime.

As the national-security scholar William Banks notes, the wall was also essential because FISA "surveillance may violate the Constitution when the FBI begins an investigation principally to build a criminal case."[19] If espionage becomes too broad, it can violate the Fourth Amendment. The original scope of FISA was carefully tailored to fit the Fourth Amendment's espionage exception. The expanded FISA, however, goes beyond and threatens to tread on Fourth Amendment rights.

The crime-espionage distinction was developed as a boundary between two very different regulatory regimes for government surveillance. This is a boundary that must be maintained. Espionage is a necessary function of government, but it is a dangerous and shadowy one, and it must remain confined lest it start polluting our constitutional democracy, where the government must be subjected to oversight and public accountability.

9

The War-Powers Argument and the Rule of Law

I n December 2005 the *New York Times* revealed that after the September 11 attacks, the Bush administration secretly authorized the National Security Administration (NSA) to engage in warrantless wiretapping of American citizens' telephone calls.[1] When they learned about this news, many Americans asked: "What is the NSA?"

Most people had never heard of the NSA. It is a secretive agency created in 1952 by President Truman to decipher encrypted foreign communications. Located in Maryland, the NSA's headquarters is known as "Crypto City." It has its own special exit off the highway, restricted to its personnel.[2] It has tens of thousands of employees and a budget in the billions. Most information about it is classified. According to James Bamford, the leading expert on the NSA, it is the "largest, most costly, and most technologically sophisticated spy organization the world has ever known."[3]

After September 11 the Bush administration directed the NSA to begin a wide-scale "Terrorist Surveillance Program," TSP for short. It listened in on international phone calls whenever NSA officials believed the calls were made to people associated with terrorist organizations. These calls included ones involving U.S. citizens. The NSA wiretapped without ever seeking a warrant or court order, disregarding the regulation and oversight required by the law.

Subsequent stories about the NSA revealed that it had obtained customer records from several major phone companies, creating the "largest database ever assembled in the world," and was conducting analysis to identify potential terrorists.[4] As the *Wall Street Journal* reported, "According to current and former intelligence officials, the spy agency now monitors huge volumes of records of domestic emails and Internet searches as well as bank transfers, credit-card transactions, travel and telephone records."[5] Although many of the NSA's activities still remain shrouded in secrecy, the short of it is that the NSA was engaging in extensive surveillance and scooping up enormous quantities of data—all with hardly any judicial oversight.

The NSA warrantless surveillance program violated the Foreign Intelligence Surveillance Act (FISA), a federal law that required judicial oversight and court orders to authorize the wiretapping. The government, however, attempted to justify the program as part of the president's power to wage war. At a congressional hearing about the program, Attorney General Alberto Gonzales testified that "the President's constitutional powers include the authority to conduct warrantless surveillance aimed at detecting and preventing armed attacks on the United States."[6] I call this the "war-powers argument," which reasons that because we're at war with foreign terrorist organizations, the president's war powers allow him to bypass the law. Congress avoided addressing the president's war-powers argument by blessing the TSP with new enabling legislation.

Some might argue that little harm was done by the program because Congress later authorized it. But in this chapter, I argue that Congress's response is quite troubling. The war-powers argument proposes an enormous and dangerous increase in executive branch power. Instead of pushing back, the legislative branch set a frightening precedent—effectively confirming that the president could break the law with little consequence. The worst part of the TSP wasn't its invasion of privacy but what it revealed about the infirmity of the rule of law.

Can the President Violate the Law?

The NSA's warrantless surveillance under the TSP was illegal. Many legal issues are ambiguous, but this one is clear. Whenever the government engages in wiretapping to gather foreign intelligence, it is regulated by FISA. FISA allows the government to engage in electronic surveillance if it obtains a court order from the Foreign Intelligence Surveillance Court, which meets in secret. The government must demonstrate probable cause that the monitored party is a "foreign power" or an "agent of a foreign power."[7] Failure to follow FISA carries civil and criminal penalties.

The law thus requires the government to get a court order to wiretap, and the NSA didn't get one. Gonzales testified to Congress why the president allowed the NSA to ignore FISA:

> The optimal way to achieve the speed and agility necessary to this military intelligence program during the present armed conflict with al Qaeda is to leave the decisions about particular intercepts to the judgment of professional intelligence officers, based on the best available intelligence information. These officers are best situated to make decisions quickly and accurately. If, however, those same intelligence officers had to navigate through the FISA process for each of these intercepts, that would necessarily introduce a significant factor of delay, and there would be critical holes in our early warning system.[8]

Translation: Going to the FISA court would have been a pain, so the NSA didn't bother. Also note Gonzales's demand for deference to security officials. As I argued in Chapter 4, such deference is unjustified, and no government official's judgments should be immune from scrutiny.

Can the president authorize the NSA to violate FISA? In a public memo, the Bush administration argued that the president has "inherent constitutional authority" as commander in chief to engage in the surveillance. The memo declared: "Among the President's most basic constitutional duties is the duty to protect the Nation from armed attack. The Constitution gives him all necessary authority to fulfill that responsibility." The memo contended that the president's broad powers to wage war trump any statute, including FISA, and it argued: "In exercising his constitutional powers, the President has wide discretion, consistent with the Constitution, over the methods of gathering intelligence about the Nation's enemies in a time of armed conflict."[9]

The problem with President Bush's argument is that its claims are far too broad. Suppose the president is right that he has the power to engage in warrantless wiretapping on his "inherent authority" as commander in chief. The implications are quite alarming. It means that the president, at his sole discretion, can secretly authorize the NSA to engage in electronic surveillance on U.S. citizens until the "War on Terrorism" is over. This is a war without a foreseeable end. Under Bush's argument, there seems to be no reason why he couldn't authorize other agencies, such as the FBI and CIA, to engage in similar surveillance. And why limit the authority to wiretaps? It could include video surveillance, bugs, document gathering, and more. The president could ignore the requirements of any law that stands in his way. If he felt that randomly shooting people was necessary to fight the War on Terrorism, he could do so in spite of murder laws. The problem with the war-powers argument is that it contains virtually no limit to the president's power.

The issue of presidential power goes to the heart of what kind of nation we will be, what kind of government we want to have. The war-powers argument says that the president can engage in activities that contravene the laws of the nation and that he can do so in secrecy, without any accountability to the people and without any oversight by the other branches of government. This is the kind of power a despot wields, not the controlled and balanced power exercised within a constitutional democracy of checks and balances.

The Need for Secrecy

When the news media reported about the NSA surveillance program, President Bush responded: "The existence of this secret program was revealed in media reports after being improperly provided to news organizations. As a result, our enemies have learned information they should not have, and the unauthorized disclosure of this effort damages our national security and puts our citizens at risk."[10]

This response is an all-too-common refrain when it comes to government programs in the name of national security—they must be kept as secret as possible. But as I argued in Chapter 7, demands for secrecy in the name of national security should be subjected to the utmost scrutiny. Keeping the very existence of the TSP secret would prevent us from having a national debate about the nature and extent of government surveillance. Central to any viable democracy is a government that is publicly accountable. The people must have the information they need to assess their government's activities.

In our democracy, the president isn't the highest power. Nor is it any bureaucrat or legislator or judge. The people are the ones in charge, and government is their servant. If the people don't know what their government is doing, then they can't hold government officials accountable. A boss can't be effective if kept in the dark.

Certainly, some degree of secrecy is necessary, especially when the government is engaged in spying. The rationale for keeping the TSP secret is that if terrorists know about the program, they might realize that their phone calls are being monitored and might stop revealing useful information. But the program was against the law, and the rule of law is what separates us from a dictatorship. It is the corner-stone of a modern democratic society, one that is run not on the whims of its leaders but according to established rules. If the Bush administration thought that FISA wouldn't be workable, then it should have immediately proposed to Congress that the law be changed. That's how things are done in a democracy.

But William Stuntz, a leading expert in criminal procedure, argues that "effective, active government—government that inno-vates, that protects people who need protecting, that acts aggressively when action is needed—is dying. Privacy and transparency are the diseases." According to Stuntz, transparency makes it harder for gov-ernment officials to act resourcefully: "For most officials most of the time, the key choice is not between doing right and doing wrong, but between doing something and doing nothing. Doing nothing is usually easier—less likely to generate bad headlines or critical blog posts."[11]

But doing nothing isn't easier for government officials. They often try to do something—the problem is that what they often try to do isn't the result of thoughtful policy analysis but a gimmicky solu-tion that will grab headlines.

Stuntz concludes his essay by observing: "We have too much privacy, and those who govern us have too little." Stuntz has it exactly backward. Transparency is what keeps the government accountable to the people. It is the only way the people can have enough infor-mation to evaluate what their government is doing and how effec-tively their government is functioning. If people are in the dark about how the government is invading their rights and liberties, then they can't reasonably assess whether the tradeoff is worth it.

Challenging the NSA Warrantless Surveillance Program

After the news of the NSA surveillance program broke, a series of lawsuits were brought to challenge the program in the courts. Some plaintiffs claimed that their constitutional rights had been violated, as well as their rights under FISA. But many courts rejected their claims, and Congress even stepped in to impede some cases.

Constitutional Rights and FISA

In one case, a group of journalists, professors, and lawyers argued that because they communicated with people who might be monitored by the NSA surveillance program, their rights under the First Amendment, Fourth Amendment, and FISA were being violated. A U.S. court of appeals threw out their case, concluding that the plaintiffs couldn't prove that they were subject to surveillance.[12] The government refused to say whether they were, and the plaintiffs were suing in part to find out. So the plaintiffs wound up being caught in a Catch-22.

The court also concluded that the plaintiffs hadn't really been injured by the NSA's failure to obtain a court order or warrant. The court reasoned that even if the NSA had obtained a warrant, the plaintiffs would never have known, since the warrants were issued in secret. "Therefore," the court reasoned, "the NSA's secret possession of a warrant would have no more effect on the subjective willingness or unwillingness of these parties to 'freely engage in conversations and correspond via email.'"[13]

The court's reasoning, however, runs contrary to the very rationale behind warrants. A warrant requires the government to justify its searches before the judiciary, a process that gives us the assurance that we can exercise our freedoms without the fear of improper government surveillance. Under our system of regulation of government searches, we cannot expect complete immunity from being subjected to a government search; but we can expect that we will not be searched contrary to established constitutional and legal procedures. If the court is right and warrants have no effect, then there would be no injury to a person if government officials sneaked into his home without a warrant, so long as he didn't find out.

But the very point of procedural regulation of government searches is to give people the assurance that they will not be searched without oversight and justification. It is the destruction of this assurance that constitutes the injury. There is a big difference between a system of highly regulated surveillance subject to oversight and limitation and a system of unregulated surveillance without oversight or limit. People might be significantly more chilled in speaking under the latter regime than under the former.

Despite the fact the TSP involved warrantless wiretapping of U.S. citizens, the court used every tool in the shed to avoid subjecting it to constitutional scrutiny.

Suing the Phone Companies

Some other people had a clever idea about how to bring the TSP to the attention of the courts. Under the Electronic Communications Privacy Act, telecommunications companies are barred from cooperating on wiretaps with government agencies in the absence of appropriate court orders.[14] Several cases were brought alleging that the phone companies broke the law by handing over information to the NSA. Since the law provides hefty civil damages for violations, successful suits would send a loud message to companies that they should follow the law rather than acquiesce to whatever demands government officials might make. Such victories would create a strong economic incentive for businesses to uphold the rule of law when the government wants to violate it. Moreover, the cases would bring more sunlight and scrutiny into the NSA surveillance program.

The government intervened and raised the state secrets privilege, thereby excluding evidence whose exposure might imperil national security. Some courts partially rejected the claims of state secrets and allowed the cases to proceed against the telecommunications companies.[15] The companies lobbied Congress for help, and in 2008 Congress responded to the TSP and to the telecom lawsuits by passing the FISA Amendments Act. The act authorizes the "targeting of persons reasonably believed to be located outside the United States to acquire foreign intelligence information." It sets forth "targeting procedures" to ensure that the collection is directed at people outside the United States. The FISA court reviews the overall procedures but not particular instances of surveillance. The act provides retroactive immunity to the telecom companies that assisted the NSA.[16] This was a huge setback for the cases brought against the companies.

The Demise of the Rule of Law

The constitutional law scholar Jack Balkin observes:

> We are not hurtling toward the Gulag or anything that we have seen before. It will be nothing so dramatic as that. Rather, we are slowly inching, through each act of fear mongering and fecklessness, pandering and political compromise, toward a world in which Americans have increasingly little say over how they are actually governed, and increasingly little control over how the government collects information on them to regulate and control them.[17]

The worst part of this story is the precedent it set. Instead of insisting the executive branch follow the law, the legislative branch was incapable of mustering any meaningful pushback. The Constitution and the laws that regulate government surveillance aim to set up a system that allows for surveillance so long as there is judicial and legislative oversight, as well as accountability. A baseline assumption that underpins these protections is that we have a government of checks and balances. But when this assumption is wrong, the system fails.

The Framers feared too strong an executive branch, in which

the president would have the powers of a king. Their idea was to divide government into three branches—the executive, the legislative, and the judicial—and have each keep the others in check and prevent them from getting too powerful. This would ensure that the rule of law would govern.

But what the events in the aftermath of the NSA surveillance program demonstrated was that the executive could boldly assert power in times of crisis and defiantly break the law, and the other branches wouldn't provide an effective check. Moreover, the executive branch could veil its actions in secrecy, preventing any accountability to the people.

The rule of law isn't self-executing—it can't work on its own. If we don't care about the rule of law, then we won't be able to maintain it. In times of crisis, a nation's true commitments are revealed. Our government failed to demonstrate a commitment to the rule of law, and this is cause for great alarm.

PART III

Constitutional Rights

How the Constitution Should

Protect Privacy

10

The Fourth Amendment and the Secrecy Paradigm

Suppose the government wants to obtain your search history from Google for the past few months. Google retains records of all the things you searched for, revealing a lot about you. You might have searched for information about stocks you own, authors you like to read, celebrities you're interested in, politicians you admire or loathe, diseases you have, information about friends or people you meet, groups and organizations you want to join, and so much more. Under the Fourth Amendment, what protection do you have?

Before I answer the question, I should point out why Fourth Amendment protection matters. The Fourth Amendment is the keystone in the protection of the citizen against government power. It ensures that the government cannot gather information about you without proper oversight and limitation. It requires that the government justify to a court why it has a compelling reason to be interested in your information.

So does the Fourth Amendment protect you when the government seeks your Google search records?

Not at all. The government can get these records from Google with a subpoena. A subpoena hardly provides any protection.[1] It's an order to produce things, but it is typically issued as a matter of course, no questions asked.

Suppose you meet a person and soon become close friends. You share a lot of information with this friend, revealing your deepest secrets. But it so happens that this person isn't your friend but an undercover cop. Does the Fourth Amendment provide protection?

Not at all.

Increasingly, the answer to whether the Fourth Amendment provides protection is "not at all." The Fourth Amendment applies only when a person has a reasonable expectation of privacy, and the U.S. Supreme Court understands privacy in a very antiquated manner. According to the Court, something is private only if it is completely secret. I call this view of privacy the "secrecy paradigm."[2] In this chapter, I explain why the secrecy paradigm is flawed and why the lack of Fourth Amendment protection for many government information-gathering activities is a big problem.

A Regulatory System in One Sentence

Unlike other countries, which have a centralized police system regulated by statute, the United States has a decentralized system of law enforcement regulated primarily by the Constitution. The structure of our current regulatory regime for government information gathering is framed largely by the Fourth Amendment, a short pronouncement which says:

> The right of the people to be secure in their persons, houses, papers, and effects, against unreasonable searches and seizures, shall not be violated, and no warrants shall issue, but upon probable cause, supported by oath or affirmation, and particularly describing the place to be searched, and the persons or things to be seized.[3]

An elaborate regulatory system rests upon this one sentence. Throngs of judicial decisions interpreting the Fourth Amendment have spawned an extensive body of rules that govern nearly all aspects

of government law-enforcement investigative activity, such as
ing in audio and visual surveillance, searching homes, cars, ba
computers, and establishing checkpoints.

The Framers of the Constitution probably had no id
the Fourth Amendment would serve as the foundation for reg
our entire system of law enforcement. They thought that the (
tution applied only to the federal government, and in 1789 t
eral government played a minimal role in law enforcement. Th
CIA, NSA, and other federal agencies did not yet exist. State an
police were also minimal, and they weren't covered by the
Amendment. But in the centuries after 1789 the nature of the (
tution and of law enforcement changed dramatically. Today th
more than 1 million full-time state and local law-enforcement
and more than 100,000 full-time federal law-enforcement off
As the number and size of police forces burgeoned, as new tec
gies gave the government greater power to gather personal in
tion, and as new federal government agencies developed to c
crime, something was needed to regulate what law-enforceme
cials could do. Comprehensive statutory regulation of law e
ment was lacking at all levels of government. So the U.S. Su
Court filled the void by crafting an extensive regulatory system
on constitutional law, and the Fourth Amendment became the
ing set of rules for when and how the government could gather
mation about individuals.

Generally—though certainly not always—the Fourth A
ment requires that government officials obtain a warrant suppor
probable cause before they can put you under surveillance or
your home or possessions. This process dictates that law-enforce
officials must go to a court and justify that they have probable
to gather your information. Probable cause is "reasonably trustw
information" that the government's search will turn up eviden
crime.[5] When the government fails to follow these procedure

typical remedy is the exclusionary rule—the information is excluded from trial.[6]

What happens when the Fourth Amendment doesn't provide protection? Sometimes, there's a statute that fills the void. But in many circumstances, there's no protection at all. There's nothing to regulate what the government can do. There's no oversight. There's nothing to limit what information it can gather or how much. There's nothing to ensure that the government is fairly targeting people it has a strong belief are guilty of a crime. There's nothing to stop law-enforcement officials from acting upon mere hunches, or even wild guesses, or just gathering information because they don't like a person and want to catch him in a bad act.

Therefore, the threshold test to determine whether the Fourth Amendment will regulate a particular government information-gathering activity becomes crucial.

When Does the Fourth Amendment Provide Protection?

What test should be used to determine when the Fourth Amendment will regulate a particular law-enforcement activity? For well over a century, the Supreme Court has wrangled with the question. The Fourth Amendment uses the terms "searches" and "seizures," but it doesn't define them. Moreover, the language of the Fourth Amendment was written centuries ago, long before modern technology dramatically altered the ways the government can gather information.

The Court's initial answer, formed in the late nineteenth century, was to focus on physical intrusions. The Fourth Amendment covered rummaging through people's papers and trespassing onto their property.[7] Such an approach made sense during this time, for this was primarily how government officials gathered information about people. But technology soon posed significant challenges to this approach.

The Case of the Whispering Wires

During Prohibition, Roy Olmstead was known as the "King of Bootleggers," and he ran a gigantic operation to import and sell alcohol on the Pacific Coast. Olmstead's empire included a fleet of ships and trucks and scores of employees. Everybody knew he was flouting the law, but he bribed the police to leave him alone.[8]

Roy Lyle, the director of the federal enforcement of Prohibition, had long wanted to nab Olmstead. The feds tapped all of the phones in Olmstead's house for about five months, generating 775 pages of notes and giving the case the nickname "the case of the whispering wires." Olmstead was convicted and sentenced to four years in prison.

Olmstead appealed, arguing that the wiretapping violated the Fourth Amendment, for it was done without a warrant. In 1928 the case made its way to the U.S. Supreme Court. In *Olmstead v. United States*, the Supreme Court concluded that the Fourth Amendment "does not forbid what was done here. There was no searching. There was no seizure. The evidence was secured by the use of the sense of hearing and that only. There was no entry of the houses or offices of the defendants."[9] The Supreme Court understood privacy violations as physical intrusions, and since the wiretapping was done through a device installed outside Olmstead's home, it didn't involve a physical trespass onto Olmstead's property.

Justice Louis Brandeis dissented. He argued that the Court's threshold test for determining Fourth Amendment coverage was myopic and antiquated. The Fourth Amendment must have the "capacity of adaptation to a changing world." A more flexible and evolving approach should be used because "subtler and more far-reaching means of invading privacy have become available to the government. Discovery and invention have made it possible for the government, by means far more effective than stretching upon the rack, to obtain disclosure in court of what is whispered in the closet."[10]

There's an interesting epilogue to the case. In 1935 President Franklin Roosevelt pardoned Olmstead. Ironically, later on, Lyle was arrested for smuggling alcohol and Olmstead testified against him.

As the *Olmstead* case demonstrated, focusing on physical intrusions was an outmoded way to determine the scope of Fourth Amendment protection. New technology enabled the government to gather a lot of private information without trespassing onto people's property or doing a physical search. Unless the Court modernized its test for determining when the Fourth Amendment would apply, the amendment would increasingly become ineffective and irrelevant.

The Gambler in the Phone Booth

Nearly forty years later, in 1967, the U.S. Supreme Court decided that it had been wrong in *Olmstead* and that wiretapping should be regulated by the Fourth Amendment. The case was *Katz v. United States*.[11] Charlie Katz lived in an apartment on Sunset Boulevard in Los Angeles. Routinely, he would use one of the three phone booths on the sidewalk outside his apartment to wager on college basketball. The FBI taped a device outside the phone booth to record his conversations. With this evidence, Katz was arrested and convicted of violating a federal statute prohibiting gambling by telephone. He was sentenced to pay a $300 fine.[12]

Katz appealed, arguing that the FBI should have obtained a warrant before recording his conversations. The government contended that under *Olmstead*, the Fourth Amendment didn't apply to the recording device since there was no physical trespass inside the phone booth. Based on the existing law, the government had the winning hand. But the Supreme Court changed the law in dramatic fashion. Whereas the Court had previously applied the Fourth Amendment only in instances involving physical trespasses, it now boldly declared: "[T]he Fourth Amendment protects people, not places.

What a person knowingly exposes to the public, even in his own home or office, is not a subject of Fourth Amendment protection. But what he seeks to preserve as private, even in an area accessible to the public, may be constitutionally protected."[13]

The Court's current approach to applying the Fourth Amendment emerges from a concurring opinion in *Katz* by Justice John Harlan. As he explained, the Fourth Amendment should regulate whenever a person exhibits an "actual (subjective) expectation of privacy" that "society is prepared to recognize as 'reasonable.'"[14] This approach is called the "reasonable expectation of privacy test."

Katz purported to usher in a wide scope of Fourth Amendment coverage. The goal of the reasonable expectation of privacy test was to permit the Fourth Amendment to respond to changing technology. As the law professor Carol Steiker observes, "Brandeis could have felt vindicated by the Court's replacement of the trespass doctrine with one more oriented toward the right of 'privacy.'"[15]

The Decline of the Fourth Amendment

Contrary to what many anticipated, the reasonable expectation of privacy test didn't broaden the scope of Fourth Amendment protection. Although the Fourth Amendment still covers searches of your home and your baggage, there are a number of instances where even physical intrusions aren't protected. For example, suppose the government trespasses onto your land, even though you put up "No Trespassing" signs. The government searches the woods on your property. Is this covered by the Fourth Amendment? No. According to the Supreme Court, "an individual may not legitimately demand privacy for activities conducted out of doors in fields, except in the area immediately surrounding the home."[16] In one case, a person enclosed his ranch with a barbed-wire fence. The police trespassed onto the ranch and looked into his barn, which had an open front. The

Supreme Court concluded that there was no Fourth Amendment protection because the ranch and the barn were exposed, and there was no reasonable expectation of privacy.[17]

The Fourth Amendment also doesn't regulate when the police search through the trash you leave out on the curb. The Supreme Court views your trash as something you have abandoned, and you've given up any expectation of privacy in things you leave behind.[18] In one case, a person shredded his documents before throwing them away, but law enforcement officials gathered them and painstakingly pieced them together. The Fourth Amendment still didn't provide any protection.[19]

Beyond physical intrusions, the Fourth Amendment doesn't apply to many kinds of surveillance. In one case, the police flew over a person's greenhouse in a helicopter and peered down through some missing roof tiles to see what was inside. The Supreme Court held that the Fourth Amendment provided no protection because the top of the greenhouse was partially exposed.[20] In another case, the government installed a tracking device on a person's car to monitor where he drove. The Court concluded that there was no Fourth Amendment protection. A "person traveling in an automobile on public thoroughfares has no reasonable expectation of privacy in his movements from one place to another."[21]

The Secrecy Paradigm

How can we make sense of all this? Using privacy instead of physical trespass was supposed to broaden Fourth Amendment protection, not constrict it. The reason privacy has led to such a narrow scope of Fourth Amendment coverage is the secrecy paradigm. The Supreme Court conceives of privacy as a form of total secrecy. Under this view, if you share your information with other people—even people you trust a lot—you can't expect privacy. If you expose your information in any way—even if the government has to go to great trouble and expense to discover it—then you can't expect privacy.

The secrecy paradigm is a very crabbed view of privacy, one that doesn't make sense in today's world. People rarely keep absolute secrets. They expect that confidants will keep their information confidential. They expect their friends not to betray them. They expect that when they're in public, they won't be followed around or secretly recorded. Even when they know others might be watching, they expect that most people won't care. When people chat in a restaurant, for example, they realize they might be overheard by nearby diners. But they also expect that the other diners won't pay much attention.

The secrecy paradigm has resulted in many forms of government information gathering falling outside Fourth Amendment protection. This is a big problem, because when the Fourth Amendment doesn't apply, there's often nothing to regulate the government. The consequence is that the government can do what it wants without any oversight or limitation.

11

The Third Party Doctrine and Digital Dossiers

In the old days, you controlled your own information. Your documents existed on pieces of paper that you possessed, and you stuffed them away in file cabinets. Your diary would be safely hidden in a dresser drawer. Dog-eared copies of the books you loved would line your bookshelves. These things were all in your home. If the government wanted to find out about your interests, hobbies, reading habits, and writings, the Fourth Amendment required a warrant to search your house.

No longer. Increasingly, through changing technology, the government can gather and use data on a massive scale in ways that end-run constitutional protection. Welcome to what is known as the "third party doctrine." According to the U.S. Supreme Court, if your information is in the hands of a third party, then you have no reasonable expectation of privacy in it—and as a result, no Fourth Amendment protection.

In the Information Age, an unprecedented amount of personal data is in the hands of various businesses and organizations. The cable company has records of what movies and television shows you watch. The phone company has data about all the phone numbers you call. Consumer reporting agencies have data about where you live, your financial accounts, and your history of paying your debts. Hospitals and insurance companies have your health data. Credit card companies have records of your purchases.

There's more. If you're on Facebook, you might have a lot of data in your profile you want only your friends to see. Google has records of all your searches going back for a while. Merchants like Amazon.com have records of everything you've ever bought with them. I'm an Amazon.com addict, and the last time I checked, I had bought more than 1,500 items over the past decade. When I survey my records there, it is like a catalog of the contents of my bookshelves and media cabinet.

With the third party doctrine, the government can now find out a lot about you without ever entering your home. Before, to find out what books you read, what movies you watched, what things you wrote, and what products you bought, law-enforcement officials would have had to enter your home and look around. But now all this information is stored with third parties. Instead of the physical copies of books people bought at the store with cash, they now have e-books in their Kindle bought online with a credit card.

And the government can get all of it—without any Fourth Amendment protection. In the digital age, the Fourth Amendment is increasingly of little relevance, and the government can access your information with hardly any oversight or limitation. In this chapter, I'll argue that the third party doctrine is one of the greatest threats to privacy in our times.

A Trip Back to the 1970s

The third party doctrine emerged in the 1970s, long before most people realized we were living in an Information Age. Computers weren't yet in widespread use. Many businesses hadn't even begun to computerize their records. It was during this time that the U.S. Supreme Court crafted the third party doctrine in a few key cases.

In 1976, in *United States v. Miller,* law-enforcement officials sought a bank customer's financial records by subpoenaing them from his bank. The banks turned over the information. The customer argued that under the Fourth Amendment, the government should have gotten a warrant before obtaining the records. But the U.S. Supreme Court disagreed, concluding that the Fourth Amendment didn't apply because the customer lacked a reasonable expectation of privacy in his bank records. According to the Court's reasoning, "the Fourth Amendment does not prohibit the obtaining of information revealed to a third party and conveyed by him to Government authorities." As the Court explained, "All of the documents obtained, including financial statements and deposit slips, contain only information voluntarily conveyed to the banks and exposed to their employees in the ordinary course of business."[1]

Three years later, the Court held in *Smith v. Maryland* that the Fourth Amendment didn't apply to pen registers—devices that recorded the phone numbers a person has dialed. Because these devices were installed at the phone company, rather than inside a person's home, and because people "know that they must convey numerical information to the phone company," they cannot "harbor any general expectation that the numbers they dial will remain secret."[2]

These cases form the backbone of the third party doctrine. If any information is exposed to a third party, then there's no reasonable expectation of privacy in it.

Digital Dossiers and the Third Party Doctrine Today

In the 1970s and early 1980s, the third party doctrine meant that you didn't have Fourth Amendment protection for your bank transactions, phone contacts, and a few other matters. But today, it means you don't have Fourth Amendment protection for most of your daily activities. That's because there are countless digital dossiers about us. A multitude of companies and organizations have amassed detailed records about our lives. Since all of these records are maintained by third parties, they fall outside of Fourth Amendment protection.

ISP Records

Suppose you're surfing the Web on your home computer. You put in some bids on eBay, buy books from Amazon.com, read articles in the *New York Times*, the *Washington Post*, and the *Wall Street Journal*. You visit a number of blogs. At these sites, you decide to post some comments, but you don't want to use your real name. So you post a review of a book at Amazon.com under the pseudonym "Avid Reader." You also post some anonymous comments to the blogs. You think your comments can't be traced to you, but they can. Amazon.com's account records link your real identity to "Avid Reader." At the blogs, your Internet protocol (IP) address is logged. An IP address is a unique number assigned to every computer online, and your Internet service provider (ISP) has records linking your identity to your IP address. Your anonymous comments can thus be traced to you by obtaining your ISP records. Does the Fourth Amendment regulate the government in obtaining this information?

Not at all. These records are held by third parties. Despite the fact only these companies have the information, and despite the fact that they don't share it with anybody, you lack a reasonable expectation of privacy in the information according to the third party doctrine.[3]

Cloud Computing

For quite a long time, we've been accustomed to having all our electronic documents and software stored on our own computers. A recent trend is to store them remotely and access them via the Internet.

An example is GoogleDocs. It allows you to store word-processing and spreadsheet documents to Google's servers, where you can jointly edit them with other people you're collaborating with. Another example is Apple's MobileMe, where you can back up the information on your iPhone—your photos, documents, contacts, and other personal data. Microsoft's SkyDrive lets you store your personal documents for free. This allows you to back up many of the important files on your computer.

The promise of cloud computing is that your documents can be much safer and your software can be always up to date. "The future," many computer experts say, "is in the cloud."

But there's a problem. Since people's documents are no longer stored on their home computers but reside instead with third parties, the shift to cloud computing will effectively remove Fourth Amendment protection from their documents.[4]

Collusion and Compulsion

There are times when companies readily cooperate with the government and will turn over your information. This happened after September 11. Government agencies went to the airlines and demanded that they surrender their customer records. Despite the fact the airlines had promised never to share their information with others, they readily handed it over.[5]

But in many instances, companies would rather not give your information to the government. They want you to trust them. Suppose you're uncertain about using a cloud computing service. The company might want to point out that it respects your privacy and will never share your information with anyone without your consent. But to be honest with you, it would have to say the following:

> We will never share your information with anyone without your consent.[*]

*Except to government officials. The government can access your data from us rather easily, and you don't have Fourth Amendment protection. If you want to retain your Fourth Amendment rights over your documents, keep them on your home computer and don't use our service.

Few companies want to make such a disclosure. Doing so might scare customers away. Perhaps there should be a warning about using cloud computing or entrusting your data to a third party. Imagine one like the surgeon general's warning about cigarettes:

WARNING: Using this service means that you'll lose your Fourth Amendment rights over your data.

A company can't meaningfully promise you confidentiality, because the government won't respect that promise. But when the government wants to promise you confidentiality, that's a different story. For example, the government spends massive sums of money trying to encourage people to fill out census forms, and there are laws protecting the confidentiality of people's answers. According to the website for the U.S. Census: "We depend on your cooperation and trust, and promise to protect the confidentiality of your information. Title 13 of the U.S. Code protects the confidentiality of all your information and violating this law is a crime with severe penalties." The site also states, "All Census Bureau employees take the oath of nondisclosure and are sworn for life to protect the confidentiality of the data." If they violate this oath, they can be fined up to $250,000 and jailed for up to five years.[6] Now that's really backing up a promise of confidentiality!

The government respects its own promises of confidentiality, yet it runs roughshod over everybody else's. Although the Fourth Amendment doesn't protect against government access to your confidential information held by third parties, the federal government has passed some statutes that provide some level of protection. Yet the protection is often quite weak. And there are no federal statutes protecting records with merchants or bookstores or many other types of businesses.[7]

Faulty Reasoning and Open Questions

The rationale for the third party doctrine comes from a series of cases involving undercover agents and informants. In these cases, the Supreme Court held that when a person tells another person a secret, she assumes the risk of betrayal. This is known as the "assumption of risk doctrine."[8]

The Supreme Court likened the third party doctrine to the assumption-of-risk doctrine. If you assume the risk that your friends will betray you, then you likewise assume the risk that third parties holding your information will betray you.

But there's a problem with this reasoning. The two situations aren't analogous. When you misplace your trust and your friend betrays you (or is an undercover agent), he voluntarily chooses to reveal your secrets. But in many instances the bank and the phone company didn't voluntarily choose to reveal people's information. They were forced to by the government. In fact, these companies often want to preserve the confidentiality of your information.

The third party doctrine fails to comprehend the concept of confidentiality—as well as the concept of a promise. If your bank promises you confidentiality, you expect it to keep its promise. If your doctor, accountant, school, or any company or organization promises you confidentiality, then you can reasonably expect that pledge to be honored. Breaching confidentiality can get one sued, and there are many circumstances under which banks, doctors, and others must pay damages if they breach confidentiality.[9] Beyond that, breaching confidentiality is bad business and can result in lost customers. So promises of confidentiality are generally respected, and people can count on them.

According to the third party doctrine, however, even a written contract isn't enough to give people an expectation of privacy. But promises and contracts are the foundation of modern civil society. If people couldn't rely on them, business and commerce would grind to a halt. Yet when it comes to privacy, the U.S. Supreme Court thinks that promises and contracts don't matter.

Another problem with the third party doctrine is that the Supreme Court has failed to clarify how far it extends. Does it have a stopping point? For example, does the third party doctrine apply to medical records? After all, people expose their medical conditions to their doctors. Would the Supreme Court really hold that people lack an expectation of privacy in their medical data because they convey that information to third parties (their physicians)? The result would strike many as absurd.

Keeping Up with Technology

Orin Kerr, a leading expert on criminal procedure, argues that the third party doctrine actually prevents technology from giving a leg up to the criminals. He contends that before the Information Age, criminals would have to do things physically—now they can do everything from their computers and better hide their tracks. The third party doctrine is needed, Kerr claims, to level the playing field.[10]

But Kerr ignores the vastly increased powers the third party doctrine gives the government. True, some criminals may use technological tools to carry out crimes. But what about the rest of us, the millions of innocent citizens who want safeguards against the government accessing our records? Just because some computer-savvy criminals can better conceal their activities shouldn't mean that we slough off all Fourth Amendment protection. Technology can help criminals, but it also can give a lot more power to the government.

Ultimately, defenses of the third party doctrine boil down to arguments that there should be no Fourth Amendment protection when the government accesses the enormous digital dossiers about us. In many instances, there's also no statutory protection. The result is that law-enforcement officials have no oversight or limitation. And that's an untenable circumstance.

The Fourth Amendment in the Information Age

The Framers of the Constitution strongly desired to protect the privacy of their documents and papers, as well as their ideas and beliefs. As their discontent with British rule grew, they began expressing their revolutionary ideas about rights and freedom and democracy, and they needed protection from British officials ransacking their homes in order to find their writings and punish them. This is why the Fourth Amendment provides a "right of the people to be secure in their persons, houses, papers, and effects, against unreasonable searches and seizures."[11]

But the Fourth Amendment has been interpreted to no longer provide such a broad right. Instead, it will provide protection against "unreasonable searches and seizures" only when your papers happen to be in your home or in your luggage. Today, information is the equivalent of one's papers. It no longer exists on fading parchment. It no longer exists within the confines of one's home or in a particular physical form. It is digital, and it resides in various computer systems maintained by third parties in distant locations.

"If you really want privacy," some argue, "just keep your data to yourself."

So don't use a credit card. Don't have cable. Don't use the Internet. Don't use the phone. Don't have a bank account. Don't have insurance. Don't go to a hospital. Don't have a job. Don't rent an apartment. Don't subscribe to any magazines or newspapers. Don't do anything that creates a record.

In other words, go live as a hermit in a cabin on a mountaintop. That's where the Fourth Amendment still protects you.

12

The Failure of Looking for a Reasonable Expectation of Privacy

In 1982, in Seattle, the nude body of a thirteen-year old girl was found, bruised and raped, dumped in a box. A teenager, John Athan, was the police's prime suspect because his brother had seen him carrying around a large box on a grocery cart near where the body was found. But the police didn't have more evidence, and the crime went unsolved.

Flash forward twenty years. With modern techniques of genetic analysis, a profile was made from DNA at the crime scene. The police searched the FBI's Combined DNA Index System, a database consisting of millions of DNA profiles from state and federal sources. No match was found.

The police recalled their initial suspicion of Athan, who had since moved away from Seattle. They wanted to find out whether the DNA profile from the crime scene matched Athan's DNA profile, but Athan's DNA wasn't in the database. The police faced a difficult problem: How would they obtain a sample of Athan's DNA? Athan surely wouldn't supply it voluntarily.

Over in New Jersey, where Athan was now living, he received a letter from the law firm Wingstrand Hargrove Kinner. He was happy to learn that he was entitled to some money. The letter stated:

Dear Mr. Athan,

A class action lawsuit has been filed against several Washington State counties and cities. These lawsuits are based on the over charging of traffic fines by local municipalities between the dates of 1987 and 1994. The records that we received indicate you may be due compensation from this over billing. The compensation may include reimbursement of fines paid, interest due and damages.

You must respond by March 21, 2003 to confirm that you wish to be included in the class membership. You may consent to be a member by signing the enclosed form and mailing by the deadline date. This form includes information we have obtained from City and County records as related to your potential claims. Please correct any discrepancies that you may find on the enclosed form so that we may correct our information.

Apparently Athan must have had a lot of parking tickets, for he responded to the letter by filling out the class-action authorization form and sending it in. The letter, however, didn't go to the firm of Wingstrand Hardgrove Kinner. The attorneys listed on the letterhead were really police officers in the Seattle Police Department. The class-action letter was just an ingenious ploy to get Athan's DNA.

When Athan's reply arrived, the police crime lab obtained his DNA from the saliva he used to seal the return envelope. The DNA profile from Athan's DNA was a match with that of the crime scene. Athan was ultimately convicted of second-degree murder.[1]

On appeal, Athan argued that the police failed to follow Fourth Amendment procedures when the officers used trickery to obtain his DNA against his wishes. How does the Fourth Amendment regulate such police tactics?

The Supreme Court of Washington held that the Fourth Amendment provides no protection at all. Athan lacked a reasonable expectation of privacy in the saliva he used to lick the envelope since he sent it away when he mailed back the reply form.[2] Indeed, DNA invariably falls outside Fourth Amendment protection. According to the U.S. Supreme Court, people lack a reasonable expectation of privacy in anything they abandon.[3]

You abandon DNA everywhere you go. Your DNA is in your hair follicles, skin cells, and saliva. If the police want your DNA, all they have to do is follow you around until you throw something away. Police have obtained DNA from discarded food, trash, and cigarette butts.[4] In one case, when a suspect refused to supply a DNA sample to the police, they obtained it when he spat on the ground—perhaps a fitting punishment for being so crude.[5]

Athan committed a despicable crime, and it is gratifying to see the police finally bringing him to justice. Some proponents of increased security point to cases like this one as prime examples of why we shouldn't want Fourth Amendment protection. But as I explained in Chapter 3, this argument relies on the all-or-nothing fallacy. We need not have a tradeoff between Fourth Amendment regulation and the police's ability to obtain and analyze a suspect's DNA. Instead of deceiving Athan into giving up his DNA, perhaps the police should have been required to obtain a warrant (or some other form of court order) for a DNA sample. This would have obviated the need for an end-run around the Fourth Amendment.

Should there be no Fourth Amendment protection for DNA? Should the police be able to use deceptive tactics without any kind of oversight? As currently interpreted, the Fourth Amendment provides protection only when courts think "privacy" is invaded. Privacy is indeed one of the key values the Fourth Amendment should protect, yet in practice, the amendment hasn't provided much protection to privacy. In this chapter, I argue that, paradoxically, the Fourth Amendment would better protect privacy if the Supreme Court stopped focusing on it.

Changing the Question

The "reasonable expectation of privacy test" currently governs the scope of Fourth Amendment protection. Ever since *Katz v. United States* was decided in 1967, the Supreme Court has determined the boundaries of Fourth Amendment protection against government information gathering by asking whether a person exhibits an "expectation of privacy" that society recognizes as "reasonable."[6]

Debates rage over whether particular government information-gathering activities invade "privacy."[7] Few commentators are particularly fond of Fourth Amendment law. Supreme Court decisions applying the reasonable expectation of privacy test have been attacked as "unstable" and "illogical"—and even as engendering "pandemonium."[8] In Chapter 9, I explained that the problem stems from the narrow and outmoded way the Supreme Court understands privacy—with what I call the "secrecy paradigm," which views privacy as total secrecy.

For a long time, I believed the fix was for the Supreme Court to adopt a more sophisticated and forward-looking view of privacy. I now realize that I was wrong. The entire debate over reasonable expectations of privacy is futile, for it is not focused on the right question. The debate is reminiscent of the philosophical dispute over a squirrel that William James relates in his book *Pragmatism:*

> The *corpus* of the dispute was a squirrel—a live squirrel supposed to be clinging to one side of a tree-trunk; while over against the tree's opposite side a human being was imagined to stand. This human witness tries to get sight of the squirrel by moving rapidly around the tree, but no matter how fast he goes, the squirrel moves as fast in the opposite direction, and always keeps the tree between himself and the man, so that never a glimpse of him is caught. The resultant metaphysical problem now is this: *Does the man go round the squirrel or not?* He goes round the tree, sure enough, and the squirrel is on the tree; but does he go round the squirrel?

James asserted that the debate was in vain—it all boiled down to what "going round" the squirrel meant. If "going round" meant passing the squirrel in all four directions, then the man went around the squirrel. But if it meant being on all four sides of the squirrel, then "the man fails to go round him, for by the compensating movements the squirrel makes, he keeps his belly turned towards the man all the time, and his back turned away." We should avoid getting bogged down in such fruitless debates, James explains, as it is more productive to focus on "practical consequences."[9]

Just as the scholars futilely debated whether the man went around the squirrel, we, too, have often been focusing on the wrong question when considering Fourth Amendment protection—whether there is an invasion of privacy. Instead, we should focus on the practical consequences of Fourth Amendment coverage. In many instances, what is or isn't protected by the Fourth Amendment bears no relation to the problems caused by government information gathering. It bears little relation to whether it is best to have judicial oversight of law-enforcement activity, what that oversight should consist of, how much limitation we want to impose on various government activities, and how we should guard against abuses of power.

There are two central questions in Fourth Amendment analysis:

1. *The Coverage Question:* Does the Fourth Amendment provide protection against a particular form of government information gathering?
2. *The Procedure Question:* How should the Fourth Amendment regulate this form of government information gathering?

The Coverage Question has preoccupied Fourth Amendment law and has led to a complicated morass of doctrines and theories. But this question should be easy to answer. We should sidestep the contentious debate about expectations of privacy—or about any other specific value as a trigger for Fourth Amendment protection.

Instead, whenever a particular government information-gathering activity creates problems of reasonable significance, the Fourth Amendment should require regulation and oversight. Such an approach would result in Fourth Amendment coverage that is comprehensive rather than haphazard. It would be consistent with the Fourth Amendment's language, which speaks broadly in terms of "unreasonable searches."

Many government information-gathering activities create problems. They invade privacy. They inhibit freedom of speech and association. They make people more frightened to explore ideas. They allow the government to amass enormous quantities of personal information, which gives government officials a vast amount of unchecked power and discretion. They can lead to abuses by law-enforcement officials. The Fourth Amendment should provide coverage whenever any of these problems might occur.

The Coverage Question thus should be easy—the Fourth Amendment provides protection whenever government information gathering causes a problem of reasonable significance. The more difficult question is the Procedure Question, which involves how the Fourth Amendment should regulate. What kind of regulation would best limit the problems created by a particular government information-gathering activity? What degree of oversight would be effective as well as practical? All the time and energy wasted on the Coverage Question should be redirected to the Procedure Question.

The Reasonable Expectation of Privacy Test

The Supreme Court has long struggled over the Coverage Question. As I described in Chapter 9, the Court used to hold that the Fourth Amendment covered only government information gathering that involved a physical trespass onto people's property or things.[10] Later on, the Supreme Court revised its test, holding that the Fourth Amendment applied whenever government information gathering infringed upon a person's reasonable expectation of privacy.[11] This new test was designed to allow the Fourth Amendment to adapt to changing technology. But the reasonable expectation of privacy test has failed to live up to aspirations. With the secrecy paradigm, the Supreme Court has held that a wide array of government information-gathering activities isn't covered by the Fourth Amendment.

The reasonable expectation of privacy test isn't merely in need of repair—it is doomed. From the way it is formulated, the test purports to be an empirical metric of societal views on privacy. The Supreme Court, however, has never cited empirical evidence to support its conclusions about what expectations of privacy society deems to be reasonable. In many instances, what the Supreme Court considers to be an invasion of privacy bears no relationship to what people have said in surveys. Christopher Slobogin and Joseph Schumacher conducted a survey to see whether people's expectations of privacy matched what the Supreme Court had determined. Their data revealed that "the Supreme Court's conclusions about the scope of the Fourth Amendment are often not in tune with commonly held attitudes about police investigative techniques."[12]

Many commentators critique the Supreme Court for failing to look to society's actual expectations of privacy. But there are good reasons for not doing so. Following polls and surveys would shackle the Fourth Amendment to the preferences of the majority. Minority groups may have different attitudes about privacy, and a goal of the Constitution is to protect minorities by limiting the will of the majority.

Another problem with looking at expectations of privacy is that technology will gradually erode what people expect to be private. As this process occurs, the government will be able to engage in ever more invasive searches and seizures. And then there's the circularity problem—expectations of privacy depend in part on the law, so a judicial decision about reasonable expectations of privacy can become a self-fulfilling prophecy.[13]

The most troublesome problem with the Supreme Court's focus on privacy is that it has led to a debate over the meaning of "privacy" and taken the focus away from the full range of problems society needs the Fourth Amendment to address. Imagine you had a choice between which of the following two government information-gathering activities should receive Fourth Amendment protection: (1) government agents at the border squeeze the outside of people's luggage without opening it; or (2) the government gathers everyone's DNA, stores it in a gigantic database, and uses it for whatever purposes it desires.

The first activity is regulated by the Fourth Amendment. In *Bond v. United States*, a border patrol agent squeezed a bus passenger's canvas bag and noticed a bricklike object that turned out to be methamphetamine. The Supreme Court held that the search violated the Fourth Amendment because bus passengers do not expect their bags to be squeezed.[14]

The second activity isn't regulated by the Fourth Amendment. As I explained earlier, DNA can readily be collected from abandoned items.

Many people would find the government obtaining their DNA—and keeping it indefinitely—to be more of a threat to privacy than a little squeeze of their luggage. Of course, some people might disagree and not view DNA as private. The problem is that this debate ignores the larger issue of whether the government should be regulated when gathering, using, and storing DNA.

A Pragmatic Approach

We should be pragmatic and recognize that when there's a problem, we should address it.[15] Problematic government information-gathering activities shouldn't be left completely unregulated. The Coverage Question thus should be a relatively easy one. The Fourth Amendment should regulate government information gathering whenever it causes problems of reasonable significance. The Fourth Amendment need not be boiled down to addressing a singular core problem. As the historian William Cuddihy has argued: "The history that preceded the Fourth Amendment . . . reveals a depth and complexity that transcend language. . . . The amendment expressed not a single idea but a family of ideas whose identity and dimensions developed in historical context."[16]

The harder question is the Procedure Question: How are particular government information-gathering activities to be regulated? Unfortunately, the Coverage Question has diverted attention from tackling the more difficult Procedure Question. This is a cop-out. The way forward is to face the Procedure Question rather than trying to avoid it.

Under this approach, the Fourth Amendment would apply to a broad range of government information-gathering activities. The tougher issues emerge with the Procedure Question: If the Fourth Amendment applies, how should a particular government information-gathering activity be regulated? As I'll explain in Chapter 13, the Fourth Amendment need not be interpreted to require a one-size-fits-all rule for all forms of government information gathering. In most cases, a particular form of oversight and regulation can be devised that will allow the government to engage in information gathering yet minimize many of the problems that are created by it.

Genetic Information and Deceptive Tactics

Let's return to the Athan case. The reasonable expectation of privacy test bogs us down in an analytical game, but the crucial problems are lost in the shuffle. The government shouldn't be able to gather people's genetic information without any oversight. It shouldn't be able to collect DNA samples without any suspicion at all. It shouldn't be able to use people's DNA however it desires and keep genetic information for however long it wants.

The benefits of using DNA identification are significant, and it certainly shouldn't be barred. But we must be mindful of the power an extensive DNA database gives the government. Since we leave trails of our DNA wherever we go, it might be possible to link particular people to particular places. That's what is done with crime scenes, but what if the use expanded beyond crime scenes? Genetic information can reveal quite a lot about a person's medical past and future, as well as information about her family members.[17] Therefore, some degree of oversight and limitation of the collection and use of this information might prevent abuses and make sure that DNA is collected only to investigate people suspected of criminal activity and not for other purposes.

Imagine if Athan had been innocent. Without Fourth Amendment protection, the police would now have his DNA. There would be no requirement that they tell him they have it, so he might never find out. There would be nothing to limit how the police might store it or use it in the future.

In addition to genetic information, the Athan case involved deceptive police tactics. It is easy to applaud the police's trickery in the case, for it helped catch a heinous criminal. But stepping back and looking at the bigger picture, the police tactics were quite troubling. Suppose the police decided to use conniving tactics more frequently. They could send you fake parking tickets to trick you into sending back a letter sealed with saliva. They could send you phony questionnaires, applications, or warranty registration forms to obtain intimate personal information. They could engage in fake psychological counseling to trick you into revealing your secrets. They could create false websites inviting you to store your documents. Every letter you received, survey you filled out, company you transacted with, website you visited, or professional you consulted could really be a ruse by law-enforcement officials to get you to turn over your personal information. Without Fourth Amendment protection, these are the tactics the government could use, and there would be no oversight.

But with Fourth Amendment regulation, many deceptive tactics would be unnecessary—the police would get the information through a warrant or court order. In cases where deception might be necessary, the courts would be able to oversee the police's activities. Sometimes, courts might not allow certain kinds of trickery that posed dangers for society. What kinds of schemes the government should be allowed to use is an issue best left to the careful consideration of the judicial branch rather than the unfettered discretion of law-enforcement officials.

In Athan's case, the Fourth Amendment should have applied. Here's how I think the Fourth Amendment should have dealt with a case like Athan's. Instead of letting the police act totally within their discretion with no oversight, the Fourth Amendment should have required the police to seek judicial authorization to obtain the DNA. If the police couldn't establish probable cause, the Fourth Amendment still should have permitted the court to authorize obtaining the DNA since the police had some evidence justifying their suspicion of Athan, the search was limited to DNA only, and there were no other viable ways to continue the investigation. If the DNA test showed Athan wasn't the culprit, then his DNA sample should have been destroyed. This approach differs somewhat from the way Fourth Amendment law currently works, and in the next chapter, I'll explain why this approach is better.

Revitalizing the Fourth Amendment

The government's information-gathering activities represent one of the most potent forms of government power—one that can affect our freedom and democracy in profound ways. Because these issues are so fundamental for the basic structure of our society, they are justifiably regulated by the Constitution.

Fourth Amendment protection *should* be broad. The amendment restricts all "unreasonable searches." Whenever the government gathers personal information and it creates a problem that isn't addressed with some form of regulation or oversight, this is unreasonable. The alternative is to allow the government to engage in activities that result in real problems, ones that invade privacy or chill speech or create the risk for abuse and other harms. The Fourth Amendment shouldn't be like a bad insurance policy, where you might find yourself unexpectedly uncovered and out of luck. The reasonable expectation of privacy test doesn't even do a good job protecting privacy, let alone all the other problems government information gathering can cause. Moving beyond the test will not only make the Fourth Amendment more responsive to these other problems, it will also improve the extent to which the amendment protects privacy.

13

The Suspicionless-Searches Argument

The School of the Americas Watch (SAW) was a group protesting the School of the Americas, a U.S. Army school in Fort Benning. Located in the city of Columbus, Georgia, the school trained foreign military leaders. SAW engaged in peaceful protests of the school, contending that it assisted dictatorships by teaching their leaders skills they used to oppress their citizens.

Led by its founder, the Rev. Roy Bourgeois, SAW held annual demonstrations outside Fort Benning, which were attended by about fifteen thousand people. In the thirteen years SAW had been organizing its protests, the protesters never possessed weapons and were never arrested for any violent acts.

But in 2002, a week before the annual protest, the city of Columbus declared that it would require all protesters to pass through a checkpoint with a metal detector. If the metal detector went off, the police would then physically search the protestor. The checkpoint would keep protestors in line about two hours before reaching the protest site. City officials instituted this security program because the Department of Homeland Security had declared the U.S. threat level to be "elevated." Once in the past, some protestors had lit a smoke bomb and a few had trespassed onto the post. And SAW invited other groups to join them, including one group that had sparked a riot a few years earlier at a meeting of the World Trade Organization.

SAW challenged the checkpoint program as a violation of the Fourth Amendment. The case made its way to the U.S. Court of Appeals for the Eleventh Circuit, which sided with SAW: "While the threat of terrorism is omnipresent, we cannot use it as the basis for restricting the scope of the Fourth Amendment's protections in any large gathering of people. In the absence of some reason to believe that international terrorists would target or infiltrate this protest, there is no basis for using September 11 as an excuse for searching the protestors." The court held that the Fourth Amendment would not allow the city "to conduct mass, suspicionless, warrantless searches." It declared:

> Indeed, it is quite possible that our nation would be safer if police were permitted to stop and search anyone they wanted, at any time, for no reason at all. Nevertheless, the Fourth Amendment embodies a value judgment by the Framers that prevents us from gradually trading ever-increasing amounts of freedom and privacy for additional security. It establishes searches based on evidence — rather than potentially effective, broad, prophylactic dragnets — as the constitutional norm.[1]

The court correctly prevented the city's officials from engaging in suspiciousness searches. Although there are exceptions, the Fourth Amendment generally requires some degree of suspicion for the government to engage in searches. Law-enforcement officials can briefly stop and frisk people, but only if they have "reasonable suspicion" that those persons are engaging in criminal activity and are carrying weapons.[2] For many searches, the Fourth Amendment requires law-enforcement officials to obtain judicial approval beforehand. For example, before the government can search your home or wiretap your phone, it must obtain a warrant. The process starts when law-enforcement officials make an application to a court. The application usually consists of an affidavit (a sworn written statement) by an official. If the judge approves the application, a warrant is issued.

A warrant must be supported by probable cause. Probable cause exists when a reasonable person would believe that a search of the designated place will turn up evidence of a crime or that the designated person has committed a crime.[3] Probable cause isn't a tremendously difficult standard to establish. Although mere hunches aren't sufficient, officials don't need certain proof. They just must have reasonable justification.

Warrant applications require law-enforcement officials to prove a legitimate basis for their suspicions. The officials must mention specific places. They can't say that they want to search everybody's home in Manhattan. Nor can the officials say that they want to search your home for "some bad stuff." They must be more specific about what they're looking for.

Increasingly, advocates for greater security contend that warrants and probable cause are impediments to the prevention of terrorism. They argue that preventing terrorism requires broad surveillance and sweeping searches to detect terrorist plotting. They maintain that requiring particularized suspicion is inconsistent with these extensive forms of information gathering. For example, Clifford May, the president of the Foundation for Defense of Democracies, argues that probable cause is "a difficult standard to meet since many of those planning terrorism have not yet committed any crime."[4] The military law scholar Glenn Sulmasy and the law professor John Yoo argue that in matters of national security "a warrant requirement becomes impractical" because of the "heightened magnitude of harm and need for swift action."[5] Many proponents of heightened security have trumpeted technologies of data mining, an issue I discuss in Chapter 19. Data mining involves gathering and analyzing extensive information about people for unusual patterns of behavior—often without any particularized suspicion.

Cases like the one involving SAW, in which courts force the government to establish particularized suspicion, are becoming rarer. Today, there are numerous exceptions to the warrant process—more than twenty by one count.[6] The U.S. Supreme Court has increasingly recognized situations involving "special governmental needs, beyond the normal need for law enforcement" where it is "impractical to require a warrant or some level of individualized suspicion in the particular context."[7] In several circumstances, the Supreme Court has even allowed random checkpoint searches.[8] As I discussed in Chapter 4, a federal court of appeals approved suspicionless searches of New York subway riders. Gradually, warrants and probable cause are becoming dinosaurs of Fourth Amendment procedure.

In this chapter, I contend that suspicionless searches should be authorized only in exceptional circumstances. Requiring law-enforcement officials to demonstrate suspicion—especially through the warrant process—is an essential way to keep their power and discretion in check. In many cases, warrants aren't inconsistent with the prevention of crime. And in circumstances where warrants truly are impractical, we must do more than just shove them aside; we must ensure that their key functions are achieved by other means.

Why Require Warrants Supported by Probable Cause?

Warrants supported by probable cause serve at least three critical functions. They limit police power and discretion, they restrict dragnet searches, and they prevent hindsight bias.

Police Power and Discretion

Warrants require a neutral and detached judge to decide whether a search is justified. They restrain police power. The police have a tremendous amount of discretion about when, where, and how to search. They can enter your home, search through your things and your computer. They can arrest you and search your body. Warrants prevent law-enforcement officials from doing these things at their mere whim, for entertainment, because they harbor personal animus toward you, because they're prejudiced against your race, religion, or ethnicity, because they don't like your beliefs or what you say, or because they don't like things you've done, or your career, or people you're friendly with.

Warrants force law-enforcement officials to believe a search is really necessary. According to the criminal procedure scholar William Stuntz: "Warrants raise the costs of searching. To get them, police must draft affidavits and wait around courthouses. Partly for this reason, warrants also raise the substantive standard applied to the search. If an officer knows he must spend several hours on the warrant, he is likely not to ask for it unless he is pretty sure he will find the evidence."[9]

We want zealous law-enforcement officials. But it's hard to ask them to be so ardent while simultaneously restraining themselves. That's why we need judicial oversight.

Warrants also prevent the police from abusing their power during a search. In one case, the police were pursuing Dominic Wilson, who had been convicted of robbery and was wanted for a probation violation. In the early morning, they burst into the home of Charles and Geraldine Wilson, Dominic's parents. The couple suddenly awakened to the noises of the police in their home. Charles Wilson, clad only in his underwear, rushed into the living room and found five men in street clothes brandishing guns. He demanded to know what was going on, and was forcefully subdued on the floor by the plainclothesmen. When the police officers realized that Dominic wasn't in the home, they left. During the entry, the police brought reporters with them as part of a ride-along program. The U.S. Supreme Court held that bringing the reporters into the Wilsons' home went beyond the scope of the warrant.[10] Warrants allow the government a limited ability to invade your home, not a license for law-enforcement officials to bring along reporters or let their friends come in to lounge on your couch and take a dip in your pool.

Dragnets

Warrants protect against sweeping dragnet investigations. A dragnet is a search conducted against a large group of people in the hopes of seeing what crimes turn up. If law-enforcement officials could search everybody's home without suspicion, they would certainly catch many more criminals. The serial killers hiding body parts in their refrigerators—caught! The drug dealers with the secret meth labs—caught! The art thieves with stolen Picassos—caught!

Although dragnet searches would turn up evidence of major crimes, they will also uncover minor offenders as well—people who have downloaded music in violation of copyright law, people in possession of small amounts of marijuana, people who have not paid taxes on items bought online. In today's world, there's so much that's criminalized. There are more than four thousand federal crimes punishable with jail time.[11] One federal judge contends that everybody is probably a criminal because such a vast amount of conduct is criminalized.[12] Another commentator argues that people commit on average three felonies per day.[13] For example, if you fail to return library books, it's a crime in Salt Lake City. If you put the U.S. flag on an advertisement within the District of Columbia, that's a crime too.[14] In addition to these odd crimes are common crimes people often commit. At some point, many parents have given their teenagers a beer—that's a violation of the law. And about half of Americans have tried illegal drugs, the possession of which is a crime.[15] Many people bet on sports—that's a crime too. The list goes on and on.

Although most of these laws are rarely enforced, they could readily be used by the government to prosecute you as a pretext if you're a persona non grata. Suppose the police do a dragnet search for drugs, but they don't find any in your house. During the search, they find out about your religious or political beliefs, and they don't like them. They also discover you've been betting on sports. They might arrest you for the illegal gambling as a pretext—just because they despise your beliefs.

Hindsight Bias

The timing of the warrant is crucial. It must be obtained *before* the government conducts the search. Why? The primary reason is hindsight bias. Suppose the police illegally search the home of a suspected terrorist and find various weapons. What judge is going to throw that evidence out because the police merely had a hunch when they did the search? Knowing the hunch turned out to be correct makes it very hard to question its validity.

This is why warrants are issued in advance. The court knows what the police know. A warrant is kind of like a gamble. The police are saying there's a decent likelihood they'll find evidence of a crime, and the judge determines whether the odds are sufficiently good. Nobody knows yet how the bet will pan out. It's very hard to make the same unbiased call when you know what happened.

In psychology, hindsight bias is a well-recognized occurrence. It is sometimes referred to as the "I knew it all along" phenomenon. Countless studies have confirmed it. In a 1991 study, people were asked to predict whether Clarence Thomas would be confirmed to become a justice on the U.S. Supreme Court. Before the Senate vote, 58 percent predicted he'd be confirmed. After he was confirmed, 78 percent claimed to have thought beforehand that he would be confirmed.[16] In another study, people were told about a train with toxic chemicals about to embark on a treacherous route through the mountains. About 33 percent said that an accident was foreseeable and the train shouldn't operate along the route. Another group of people were told that the train had taken the route, derailed, and spilled toxins into a river. About 66 percent of this group said that the accident was foreseeable and the train shouldn't have operated along the route.[17]

When you know something in hindsight, you're more likely to think that you could have predicted it all along. Hindsight bias is difficult to eradicate. Even when people are told to ignore the actual outcome and imagine that they don't know what has happened, they can't do so effectively.[18]

Does the Process Work?

Are Warrants Merely a Rubber Stamp?

Courts issue warrants quite frequently, and this fact might suggest they are just a rubber stamp rather than a meaningful form of protection. But far from demonstrating that the warrant system isn't working well, the high rate of warrants granted shows that law-enforcement officials most often refrain from making spurious search requests to courts. Officials must build trust with judges, for they keep coming back to the same judges for warrants in other cases. If a judge loses faith and stops authorizing warrants, his recalcitrance could impede future investigations.

Indeed, in the vast majority of cases, the police find what they're looking for. More than 80 percent of the time, they find at least some of the evidence they predicted they'd find.[19] This success rate illustrates that warrants aren't being granted too liberally.

Can Warrants Work for Prospective Threats?

As I have mentioned, some commentators argue that warrants and probable cause are designed primarily for investigation rather than prevention. But the warrant and probable-cause require-ments are not incompatible with surveillance designed to detect pro-spective threats. The requirement would prohibit surveillance based upon mere conjecture, naked suspicion, race or nationality, religious affiliation, or political speech. It would not, however, require that the government investigate only crimes already concluded. The planning of future crimes, especially terrorism, is itself a crime. Laws against conspiracy criminalize the making of an agreement to commit an il-legal act. Taking the initial steps to commit a crime, such as obtaining materials for it or scoping out the scene, itself constitutes the crime of attempt. Therefore the government could obtain a warrant to engage in electronic surveillance if it had "reasonably trustworthy information" that a future crime was being planned or discussed by conspirators.

A Reasonableness Standard?

The legal scholar Akhil Amar argues that the Fourth Amend-ment has long been misinterpreted to require the use of warrants sup-ported by probable cause for searches and seizures. Amar contends the Fourth Amendment merely requires "reasonableness."[20] In other words, so long as the government is acting reasonably in what it is doing, then the demands of the Fourth Amendment are satisfied.

A pure reasonableness standard would be problematic. As the criminal procedure expert Anthony Amsterdam laments, there's a "general ooziness" to the reasonableness standard.[21] Reasonableness is quite amorphous—it has no focus. In practice, it has been rather toothless, and it lacks guiding principles.[22] The nebulous nature of reasonableness cannot adequately constrain police discretion. More-over, reasonableness is frequently determined after the searches have occurred or are under way, leaving the determination vulnerable to the problem of hindsight bias.

Beyond Warrants and Probable Cause

There should be a strong presumption for a warrant and probable cause. There are circumstances, however, under which requiring a warrant and probable cause will hinder law-enforcement activities. For example, if warrants and probable cause are required too frequently, a Catch-22 will be created: The police need to find enough evidence to get probable cause, yet they might not be able to obtain it because they didn't have enough probable cause to get a warrant. In other words, the police need to be able to do some investigating before the Fourth Amendment requires a warrant and probable cause.

Suppose the police get an anonymous tip that you're dealing drugs. The police can't search your home without a warrant, and the Supreme Court has ruled that while a reliable informant is sufficient for probable cause, an anonymous tip isn't.[23] The police need more evidence, something to corroborate the tip. At this point, the police might follow you around, search your trash, or obtain records from third parties—none of which is currently regulated by the Fourth Amendment. Earlier I argued that these activities should be covered by the Fourth Amendment. But if they are, and a warrant and probable cause are required to engage in these kinds of information gathering, then the police might be stuck, unable to gather more evidence to corroborate the tip.

Under certain circumstances, this problem might justify a deviation from the warrant and probable-cause requirements. A stepladder authorization process might work. The police could present the court with their evidence. If it is sufficient to constitute probable cause, the police could obtain a warrant. If it isn't sufficient for probable cause, the court could consider authorizing one further investigatory step. Law-enforcement officials would demonstrate evidence beyond mere speculation and propose limited measures to obtain more information to corroborate the evidence they have. The court would then determine whether they have sufficient justification to continue on to the next step in their investigation, such as going through your trash.

In some instances, the government might want to engage in broader forms of surveillance when they don't have any particular suspects in mind. Courts should view such requests with great skepticism and should require the government to justify why a warrant and probable cause should not be required. If the government can justify its surveillance measures, and such measures have reasonable limits and are not mere attempts to fish around for wrongdoing based on speculation, then courts should grant approval. Any deviation from the warrant and probable cause requirement should ensure the following:

1. Searches should be as limited as possible.
2. Dragnet searches should be restricted.
3. Searches conducted without warrants and probable cause must be done only when there are no other alternatives.
4. The government must prove convincingly why the searches are impractical with a warrant or probable cause.
5. The value of conducting the search without a warrant or probable cause must outweigh the harms caused by the search, such as invasion of privacy and the chilling of speech, association, and religion.
6. Mechanisms must be in place to ensure that people's rights are adequately protected and that law-enforcement officials don't abuse their discretion.
7. The government should be required to delete unused information after a certain period of time.[24]

14

Should We Keep the Exclusionary Rule?

I was once a juror in a burglary case. A man entered a school building and was hovering around, looking suspicious, holding an empty attaché bag. He was confronted by a security guard and asked what he was doing in the building. He said he was selling magazine subscriptions, but he didn't have any magazines, brochures, or sign-up sheets. He didn't even have anything to write with. The security guard called the police, and the man was arrested and charged with burglary.

To be guilty of burglary, the man had to have unlawfully entered the building with the intent to commit a crime. We acquitted him of burglary. We didn't think there was enough evidence to conclude that his intent was to commit a crime, though we all felt in our gut he was up to no good. We wished we had more evidence, something to give us a better idea of why he was wandering around the building. We thought that more likely than not he was trying to steal something, but to convict someone, the prosecution had to prove its case beyond a reasonable doubt, and it fell short.

After the trial, I had a chance to speak with the prosecutor, who told me that a key piece of evidence was excluded. Inside the man's bag was a set of burglar's tools. That fact was kept from the jury based on the "exclusionary rule," which works by barring evidence at trial when the government gathers it by violating the Fourth Amendment. In this case, the police hadn't searched the man's bag properly under the Fourth Amendment, so the prosecutor couldn't use the evidence of the burglar's tools. Had I known about the tools, I surely would have voted to convict, and I have no doubt the other jurors would have done so as well. The result of the exclusionary rule was that a guilty man wasn't convicted. Is this too high a cost for ensuring that the Fourth Amendment is followed?

The exclusionary rule is the primary way of enforcing the Fourth Amendment. The rule ensures that the government respects Fourth Amendment rights, but it comes at a great price. In the movies or on TV, whenever you see a sneering criminal striding out of the courtroom while the police gripe about "technicalities," this is probably the exclusionary rule at work.

The exclusionary rule has produced a vigorous debate. Hardly anybody likes the rule; even its supporters find it ugly. Nevertheless, privacy proponents strongly defend the rule, arguing that it is a necessary evil and better than the alternatives.[1]

Is the exclusionary rule the best way to guarantee that the government follows the Fourth Amendment? For a long time, I thought yes. Now, I think no. In this chapter, I'll explain my change of heart.

Searching Dolly Mapp's House

How did the exclusionary rule come into being? It had long existed, but it wasn't until 1961 that the U.S. Supreme Court mandated the rule for Fourth Amendment violations.[2] In that year, the Supreme Court confronted a case involving outrageous conduct by the police.[3]

Dollree ("Dolly") Mapp was a twenty-eight-year-old African-American woman living in a house with her daughter when three police officers arrived at her door. Earlier, a bomb had blown up the house of Don King (who later became a well-known boxing promoter). The police were on the trail of a suspect, and they saw a car belonging to a man associated with the suspect parked in Dolly's driveway. The officers banged on the door and demanded to come inside and search. Dolly talked to them through the window. After calling her lawyer, Dolly told the police that he had advised her not to let them inside without a warrant.

Four more police officers arrived. They continued to knock on the door, but Dolly refused to answer. So they broke in through the back door. Furious, Dolly confronted them and demanded to see a warrant. One of the officers held up a piece of paper. Dolly snatched it and stuck it in her bosom. The officers then grabbed her, pulled the paper away, and handcuffed her. They then searched the house. They found no evidence of any bombing. But they did find some porno-graphic pamphlets they thought were obscene, so they arrested Dolly on suspicion of violating obscenity laws.

At trial, Dolly argued that the pamphlets the police seized shouldn't be allowed into evidence. The search of Dolly's home was clearly a violation of the Fourth Amendment. The police needed a valid warrant to search Dolly's home, and they didn't have one. The piece of paper that the police flashed before Dolly wasn't a warrant. In fact, it mysteriously vanished before trial.[4]

The case eventually made its way to the U.S. Supreme Court. In *Mapp v. Ohio,* the Court concluded that evidence found in viola-tion of the Fourth Amendment must be excluded from trial. The Court reasoned that the exclusionary rule was necessary to ensure that the government show proper respect for the Fourth Amendment. "Noth-ing can destroy a government more quickly than its failure to observe its own laws, or worse, its disregard of the charter of its own existence."[5]

The idea behind the exclusionary rule is that it wipes out vio-lations of the Fourth Amendment as if they never happened. For Dolly Mapp, since the police learned about the pamphlets only be-cause they violated the Fourth Amendment, they shouldn't get to use them against her.

The *Mapp* opinion, making the exclusionary rule the law of the land, sparked an immediate outcry. The New York City police commissioner declared that the exclusionary rule would have a "traumatic effect" on the law, akin to "tidal waves and earthquakes."[6] Controversy has surrounded the rule ever since.

There is an interesting epilogue to Dolly's case. After her Supreme Court victory, she moved to New York. Many years later, the police conducted a search of her home because they suspected her of receiving stolen property. This time, they found what they were looking for—stolen electronics and antiques. They also found fifty thousand envelopes of heroin. Unlike the police search before, the New York police had a search warrant. They knew they had to get one—and they probably knew it so well because of Dolly Mapp's case. Dolly was convicted and sentenced to twenty years in jail.

Why Have the Exclusionary Rule?

The Fourth Amendment doesn't say anything about how it is to be enforced. It just says that searches and seizures shouldn't be unreasonable and that warrants must be supported with probable cause. The amendment's text says nothing about what happens if it is violated. A rule without a remedy is like a bee without a stinger. It can readily be ignored. This is why the Fourth Amendment needs an enforcement mechanism, and the exclusionary rule has filled this role for the past half-century. And in truth, the exclusionary rule has many virtues.

Fairness

At the most basic level, the rule seems simple and fair: If you get something by breaking the rules, then you shouldn't get to keep it and benefit from it. You should give it back. And that's what the exclusionary rule does. The government shouldn't be able to profit from its own wrong, and the exclusionary rule is a form of restitution—it gives the evidence back to the defendant from whom it was unlawfully taken. There's a nice sense of propriety to the exclusionary rule, for it tries to restore things to what they would have been had the government not violated the Fourth Amendment.

Deterrence

The primary argument supporting the exclusionary rule is that it serves as a good deterrent against violating the Fourth Amendment. If police know that anything they obtain by violating the Fourth Amendment will be worthless, there's no reason to get it improperly. Law-enforcement officials want to have criminals convicted. Violating the Fourth Amendment impedes this goal. So the exclusionary rule gives the police a strong incentive to follow the proper Fourth Amendment procedures. In Dolly Mapp's case, for example, the police could have obtained a valid warrant before searching her home. Had they done so, they could have used what they found. The exclusionary rule makes clear that their warrantless search of Dolly's home was a waste of time.

Incentive to Litigate

An additional virtue of the exclusionary rule is that it gives defendants an incentive to stand up for Fourth Amendment rights. When the government violates the Fourth Amendment, there are no consequences unless someone complains. If defendants wouldn't get a benefit for complaining about Fourth Amendment violations, then they wouldn't bother. The exclusionary rule entices defendants to bring Fourth Amendment violations to the attention of courts and to litigate them.

The Problems with the Exclusionary Rule

I've long believed the conventional wisdom and embraced the exclusionary rule. But I've increasingly soured on it. Despite the rule's virtues, its vices now strike me as too significant to tolerate.

Penalty for All of Society

The exclusionary rule penalizes not just the police but all of society. As Judge Benjamin Cardozo famously warned, with the exclusionary rule, the "criminal is to go free because the constable has blundered."[7] If the police make a mistake and violate the Fourth Amendment and a serial killer is set loose, everybody suffers, not just the police.

In practice, though, only a handful of criminals actually go free because of the exclusionary rule. In most cases, it excludes only a few pieces of evidence, and there's plenty left to convict the criminals.[8] Although the exclusionary rule rarely sets criminals free, it sometimes leads to shorter prison sentences. Faced with important evidence being excluded, prosecutors are willing to strike more lenient plea-bargain deals with defendants. But this result probably isn't significant enough to deter Fourth Amendment violations.

Empirical studies are mixed on the exclusionary rule's deterrent effect, with many studies showing that the rule doesn't adequately deter.[9] As the legal scholar Christopher Slobogin observes, the rule not only fails to deter but also undermines respect for the judiciary when evidence is excluded.[10] The rule thus helps defendants at society's expense.

Lack of Proportionality

The exclusionary rule lacks any sense of proportionality. No matter whether the tainted evidence points to a heinous crime or a minor infraction, the exclusionary rule works like a cleaver, chopping off evidence without any balance or consideration of the costs.

Imagine a terrorist plans to destroy New York City with a dirty bomb. The police search the terrorist's home and find bomb components. But they make a minor blunder, and as a result, the search is invalid. With the exclusionary rule, the evidence will be excluded, even though the terrorist could have annihilated an entire city. Preventing the Fourth Amendment violation hardly seems worth the cost of excluding the evidence.

Remedy for the Guilty

Suppose the police illegally search a person's home. They find nothing. Because the person is innocent, there won't be a trial and there won't be evidence to exclude. The exclusionary rule does nothing to remedy the invasion of privacy to the innocent person or the embarrassment and anxiety of having the police swarm all over his house.

Now suppose the police find a horde of stolen items in the person's house. The person is tried for robbery. This time, he can use the exclusionary rule. Ironically, if he's innocent, the exclusionary rule is of no help. If he's guilty, then the rule is very helpful.

Shrunken Scope of Fourth Amendment Protection

The worst problem with the exclusionary rule is that it has decimated the Fourth Amendment. As Judge Guido Calabresi has argued, "the exclusionary rule, in my experience, is most responsible for the deep decline in privacy rights in the United States."[11] Judges don't like to exclude evidence from trial. Because the consequences of finding a violation are so grave, an easy escape is just not to find a Fourth Amendment violation. The exclusionary rule thus encourages courts to keep the Fourth Amendment's coverage as narrow as possible.

The criminal procedure expert Yale Kamisar contends that "a down-sized Fourth Amendment that is taken seriously is still a good deal better than an expansive majestic Fourth Amendment that exists only in the theoretical world."[12] But the problem with his view is that the current Fourth Amendment is so downsized that it isn't taken seriously. It is so narrow in its protection that it leaves far too much unregulated.

Moreover, the exclusionary rule makes people loathe the Fourth Amendment. They see criminals benefit as a consequence of Fourth Amendment protections and lose respect for these rights. Judges who throw out evidence based on Fourth Amendment violations are castigated as pariahs, not celebrated as heroes who enforce our constitutional rights.

Toward a Solution

I've now reached the conclusion that the exclusionary rule causes tremendous problems and is, on balance, a bad way to enforce the Fourth Amendment. A combination of measures would probably serve as a viable alternative. Before discussing the solutions, it is important to understand the key things that an enforcement remedy for the Fourth Amendment must do:

1. *Deter.* A Fourth Amendment remedy must adequately deter violations. It must be something that police officers dislike enough to make them comply with the Fourth Amendment.
2. *Show respect.* A remedy must show proper respect for the Fourth Amendment. If the remedy is something minor, then we are saying that Fourth Amendment rights aren't important. The

sanction for violating the Fourth Amendment must be severe, for it must reflect that people's rights really matter.

3. *Incentivize.* There must be an incentive for defendants to challenge Fourth Amendment violations. Otherwise, law-enforcement officials will realize that they can ignore the Fourth Amendment because few will stand up and demand that they follow it.

I propose the following bundle of measures:

Deterrence and Training

To deter Fourth Amendment violations, courts should order remedial Fourth Amendment training programs for law-enforcement officials guilty of violations, who must then pass a test to graduate from the training. Officials won't relish spending days in training and preparing for an exam. Remedial training programs will probably deter violations more than the exclusionary rule. As one study revealed, police departments often fail to notify officers when courts hold that their searches violated the Fourth Amendment. The authors of this study also quizzed the officers about what was allowed and forbidden by the Fourth Amendment. The officers got little more than half of the questions correct. The study's authors concluded: "Officers cannot be deterred from engaging in illegal conduct if they do not understand what is illegal."[13] In contrast to the exclusionary rule, training programs will deter violations as well as instruct law-enforcement officials about the rules they must follow.

External Supervision

Police departments and federal law-enforcement agencies must have an incentive to train officers and promote respect for the Fourth

Amendment. To create this incentive, courts should appoint an independent expert to investigate and supervise any law-enforcement organization with a high percentage of violations for its size in a given year. Once the percentage of violations drops below a certain threshold, the judicial supervision should cease. Because law-enforcement organizations will want to avoid external supervision ordered by courts, this measure will encourage them to improve their own internal supervision.

Transparency and Accountability

All violations should be tallied and publicized. Currently, we know little about the extent of Fourth Amendment violations. Keeping track of violations will make it possible to compare rates among police departments, and will foster greater accountability.

Rewards for Compliance

Currently, there's little reward for law-enforcement officials to respect Fourth Amendment rights, but there are many rewards to zealously investigate crime. The rewards need to be more balanced. Law-enforcement officials with good Fourth Amendment compliance should be given bonuses and commendations.

Fines

There must be an incentive for defendants to litigate. Fourth Amendment violations should be penalized via a fine paid to defendants by police departments or government law-enforcement agencies. The amount should be imposed by judges rather than by juries, which might be unlikely to award damages to criminals. There should be a minimum amount for the fine—a sum with some heft, though not extravagant—as well as attorney's fees to incentivize the lawyers to work hard to litigate the issue. The fine should be greater for willful violations than for negligent ones.

Bad Faith

Although most cases shouldn't involve the exclusion of evidence, the exclusionary rule should still be imposed in limited circumstances. When a court finds that law-enforcement officials violated the Fourth Amendment in bad faith, exclusion should be the presumptive remedy, since bad-faith violations are less responsive to fines or training. *Mapp*, for example, involved bad faith. The police knew they needed a warrant and didn't have one, so they held up a piece of paper pretending it was a warrant. They knew better but didn't care. Exclusion was a proper remedy in that case. On the other hand, for negligent violations or in circumstances when Fourth Amendment rules aren't clear, the evidence shouldn't be excluded.

Unlike the United States, many countries have a discretionary rather than a mandatory exclusionary rule. Judges have a choice about whether to exclude evidence. In England and Australia, for example, courts are likely to exclude evidence when the police violate clear rules but to allow it when the rules aren't clear. Canada also has a discretionary exclusionary rule. Germany, too, uses a discretionary exclusionary rule, balancing privacy rights against "society's interest in having all relevant evidence presented."[14] Professor Craig Bradley extensively studied the approaches of various countries to the exclusionary rule, and he concluded that "a discretionary system can work as long as it is based on clear, codified rules and taken seriously by the courts, particularly the nation's highest court."[15]

Abandoning the Exclusionary Rule

Grudgingly, the exclusionary rule has long been accepted as necessary to enforce the Fourth Amendment. But the rule doesn't work as well as many people presume. Instead of encouraging respect for constitutional rights, the exclusionary rule makes the police and public antagonistic toward the Fourth Amendment. It is time to reexamine the conventional wisdom and move beyond the exclusionary rule.

15

The First Amendment as Criminal Procedure

Suppose law-enforcement officials want to learn about your political beliefs, religion, reading habits, or what you write and say to others. They seek records of the books you bought from Amazon.com. They demand from Facebook a list of the people you communicate with. How much protection do you have when the government tries to conduct these searches?

Usually, the answer comes from a field of law called criminal procedure. As I've discussed in previous chapters, the Fourth Amendment to the U.S. Constitution regulates how the government can gather information about you, and it currently fails to provide you with much protection.

But these searches also affect your First Amendment rights. The First Amendment contains a broad constellation of rights, including freedom of speech, association, thought, and belief.[1] Knowing that the government is gathering information about you can inhibit you from exercising your First Amendment rights. Does the First Amendment provide protection?

The question is rarely asked. Lawyers and judges generally don't think of the First Amendment as relevant to criminal procedure. In law schools the First Amendment and the Fourth Amendment are taught in different classes. They are understood as separate domains of law, having little to do with each other.

In this chapter, I argue that the First Amendment should be considered alongside the Fourth Amendment as a source of criminal procedure. This is a bold new role for the First Amendment, but as I hope to demonstrate, it's a role that fits.

A Common History

The First and Fourth Amendments share a common history. They were inspired by government inquests into speech, religion, belief, and association.[2] For example, prosecutions for seditious libel were frequently used in Britain in the eighteenth century to suppress criticism of the government, and there were well over a thousand seditious speech prosecutions in the colonies.[3] A few of these cases strongly influenced the Framers. In particular, John Peter Zenger was tried for seditious libel in 1735 in colonial New York, and a jury nullified the law in order to acquit him.[4] The Zenger case, in the words of one commentator, served "as a crucible for the flames of liberty and freedom of the press that were stirring in the Colonies."[5]

Another case in England, *Wilkes v. Wood*, also generated an enormous buzz in the colonies.[6] A notorious figure of his time, John Wilkes was a libertine, always in debt, constantly enmeshed in quarrels, and often engaging in duels. He liked to drink—quite a lot—and he loved the company of mistresses and courtesans. Known as one of the ugliest people alive, he was losing his teeth by the age of thirty. He divided his time between sitting in Parliament and in the Tower of London.[7]

But Wilkes became an unlikely hero, one of the great champions of liberty. Between 1762 and 1763 Wilkes published a series of anonymous pamphlets titled *The North Briton*, including an issue number 45 that sharply criticized the king.[8] Armed with a general warrant authorizing a search for anything connected to *The North*

Briton number 45, government officials searched Wilkes's home, seized his papers, and arrested him.[9] Such general warrants were common at the time and were used to muzzle the press and squelch political dissent.[10]

Wilkes sued to challenge the general warrant. At trial, Chief Justice Pratt instructed the jury that if the government had the power to use general warrants, "it certainly may affect the person and property of every man in this kingdom, and is totally subversive of the liberty of the subject."[11] The jury found for Wilkes, and the case became the stuff of legend. It was seen as an enormous victory for freedom of the press, and the British press ensured that news about the case was spread far and wide. The number "45" was etched in chalk throughout London, and Benjamin Franklin noted after a visit that he observed a fifteen-mile stretch where "45" was marked on practically every door.[12] Hailed as a hero in Britain, Wilkes became a champion in the American colonies as well.[13]

Two years after the *Wilkes* case, John Entick challenged a general warrant in a seditious libel investigation. As with Wilkes, Entick's home had been searched and his papers seized. In *Entick v. Carrington*, Lord Camden (formerly Chief Justice Pratt, the author of the *Wilkes* opinion) issued a blistering critique of general warrants.[14] Camden declared that with a general warrant, a person's "house is rifled; his most valuable secrets are taken out of his possession, before the paper for which he is charged is found to be criminal by any competent jurisdiction, and before he is convicted either of writing, publishing, or being concerned in the paper."[15] Word of the *Entick* case was also greeted with cheer in the colonies, and Wilkes and Lord Camden were so venerated that towns were named in their honor, such as Wilkes-Barre, Pennsylvania, and Camden, New Jersey.

As the criminal procedure expert William Stuntz observes, the Fourth Amendment emerges from "a tradition that has more to do with protecting free speech than with regulating the police."[16]

Criminal Procedure and First Amendment Rights

The Need for First Amendment Protection

Government information gathering can threaten one's ability to express oneself, communicate with others, explore new ideas, and join political groups. Without protection against government probing, countless conversations might never occur or might be carried on in more muted tones. Government probing can lessen the effectiveness of democratic participation by depriving speakers of anonymity, which can be essential for candid speech. The U.S. Supreme Court has held that protecting anonymity is necessary to foster speech about unpopular views: "Persecuted groups and sects from time to time throughout history have been able to criticize oppressive practices and laws either anonymously or not at all."[17]

In addition to protecting speech, the First Amendment safeguards intellectual inquiry.[18] Government information gathering can make people reticent to read controversial books or investigate unpopular viewpoints. Freedom of association can also be quelled by governmental invasions of privacy. People may be reluctant to join certain groups if the government is recording membership information.[19] And freedom of the press can be compromised when the government subpoenas journalists to reveal confidential sources. Government information gathering can thus strike at the heart of First Amendment rights.

Fourth Amendment protection has receded in precisely those areas most important to First Amendment rights. As a result, the government can readily use subpoenas to gather information pertaining to communications, writings, and the consumption of ideas.[20] Subpoenas are often issued without judicial approval, without a requirement of probable cause, and without many limitations.[21] As Stuntz notes, Ken Starr used subpoenas much more than warrants in his investigation of President Bill Clinton:

This use of the grand jury and its power to subpoena, rather than the police and their power to search, gave Starr's team the authority to find out just about anything it might have wanted. For while searches typically require probable cause or reasonable suspicion and sometimes require a warrant, subpoenas require nothing, save that the subpoena not be unreasonably burdensome to its target. Few burdens are deemed unreasonable.[22]

As I discussed a few chapters ago, the Supreme Court has held that the Fourth Amendment doesn't cover instances when a person's information is gathered from third parties. Unfortunately, the Fourth Amendment focuses not on what various records or documents can reveal but on where they are located or who possesses them.[23] In the past, personal papers and correspondence were often located in people's homes, which have always received strong Fourth Amendment protection. People's conversations would take place in private places or through sealed letters, shielding them from government access without a warrant. Today, however, Internet surfing in the seclusion of one's home creates data trails with third parties in distant locations. First Amendment activity is no longer confined to such private zones as the home and thus no longer benefits from Fourth Amendment protection.

Therefore, because the Fourth Amendment doesn't adequately protect against government information gathering that implicates First Amendment activities, the First Amendment should serve as an independent source of criminal procedure.

When Should the First Amendment Provide Protection?

The government can violate the First Amendment even without directly prohibiting First Amendment activities. The Supreme Court has noted that the First Amendment restricts the government from creating a "chilling effect" on freedom of speech, association, belief, or receipt of ideas.[24] Courts have concluded that government information gathering indirectly inhibits or "chills" First Amendment liberties in a wide range of contexts, including surveillance of political activities, identification of anonymous speakers, prevention of the anonymous consumption of ideas, discovery of associational ties to political groups, and enforcement of subpoenas to the press or to third parties for information about reading habits and speech.[25] For example, you might not want to purchase a book if it will be used against you in a trial for conspiracy to engage in a crime.[26] You might not visit religious or political websites if you knew that the government might use this as evidence against you. Even without criminal charges, the fear that speaking or reading certain things might trigger an arrest or a criminal investigation might be sufficiently daunting to inhibit you.

Criminal investigations and prosecutions aren't the only potential sources of chilling effects. In many instances, the government engages in broad information gathering that isn't directly tied to a concrete penalty but which still may chill speech. For example, the government could create a terrorist watch list based on people's speech or associations, yet individuals might never know whether they're on the list. Or the government could amass information about people's speech and reading habits in a gigantic database for some unknown future use. Although in these instances it would be difficult for you to prove the government collected information about you, the First Amendment doctrine of overbreadth would allow you to raise a challenge if the government's actions were needlessly broad and threatening to many people's rights.[27] A government information-gathering program that sweeps in a great deal of First Amendment activity will be deemed unconstitutionally overbroad if not narrowly tailored to a substantial government interest.

What Level of Protection Should the First Amendment Require?

When the First Amendment applies, government information gathering would be upheld only if it served a substantial government interest and employed narrowly tailored means to achieve that interest. The First Amendment would rarely completely ban a particular instance of government information gathering. If the government interest is substantial, the First Amendment would mandate procedures that must be followed for the information gathering to take place. These procedures would be similar to those required by the Fourth Amendment. In many instances, the First Amendment would require law-enforcement officials to obtain a warrant supported by probable cause.

A New Role for the First Amendment

For far too long, courts and commentators have viewed the First Amendment as irrelevant to criminal procedure. But as Fourth Amendment protections recede from those areas where First Amendment activity is most likely to occur, it is time to look to the First Amendment for protection. First Amendment criminal procedure is both justified and necessary to prevent the infringement of First Amendment rights in the course of government investigations. It is time for the First Amendment to take its place alongside the Fourth Amendment as a source of criminal procedure.

PART IV

New Technologies
How the Law Should Cope with
Changing Technology

16

Will Repealing the Patriot Act Restore Our Privacy?

oon after the September 11 attacks in 2001, Congress passed the Uniting and Strengthening America by Providing Appropriate Tools Required to Intercept and Obstruct Terrorism Act—a clunky title designed to produce the acronym USA PATRIOT.[1] The statute is most commonly referred to as the Patriot Act.

The Patriot Act was a grab bag of tweaks to existing electronic-surveillance law. Ironically, most of its changes weren't directly linked to September 11. Much of the act was rehash—a series of proposals the Department of Justice (DOJ) had previously failed to get Congress to pass. After September 11, with Congress eager to do something, Attorney General John Ashcroft asked the DOJ for recommendations. The DOJ dusted off its proposals, and they were sent over to Congress.[2] This time, Congress was more receptive.

The act was controversial, quickly becoming the nucleus of the debate between privacy and security. In his documentary *Fahrenheit 9/11*, Michael Moore accused many members of Congress of failing to read the act before voting on it. "The only patriotic thing to do," he resolved, "was for me to read it to them." He proceeded to read the act from a loudspeaker while driving around the Capitol in an ice cream truck.[3]

The passage of the Patriot Act has often been characterized as a watershed event that eviscerated privacy rights. I've spoken to countless people about the act, and they invariably lament that the act killed privacy. Their view seems to be that before the act, we had strong privacy rights against government surveillance, which the act eviscerated.

But all the hoopla has been focused too much on the Patriot Act itself and not enough on the law more generally. Many of the complaints about the Patriot Act relate to problems with the law that existed long before the act was ever passed.

Suppose the Patriot Act were repealed tomorrow. Would privacy be restored? In many circumstances, not at all. Certainly, the Patriot Act has problematic features, but it's just the tip of a much larger iceberg.[4] Many of the problems attributed to the Patriot Act existed in electronic-surveillance law for quite a while. In this chapter, I argue that the problems with electronic surveillance didn't begin with the Patriot Act, and that they won't end with it either. We must rethink electronic-surveillance law as a whole.

Did the Patriot Act Reduce or Expand Internet Privacy?

Many critics of the Patriot Act decried its reduction of Internet privacy for email and Web surfing. Defenders of the act claimed that it actually expanded privacy protection. Someone must be wrong, right? Actually, they're both correct to some degree.

There's no way to understand what's going on without understanding how electronic-surveillance law worked before the Patriot Act. The act wasn't written on a blank slate. A lot of law already regulated electronic surveillance. First, there was the Fourth Amendment. When the Fourth Amendment protects something, it provides a high level of protection (in many cases, requiring a warrant supported by probable cause). A statute can't supply less protection, but it can always supply more.

In addition to the Fourth Amendment, a set of statutory provisions protected against electronic surveillance—the Electronic Communications Privacy Act (ECPA), which consists of three statutes bundled together: the Wiretap Act, the Stored Communications Act, and the Pen Register Act. These statutes regulate different aspects of electronic surveillance and provide different levels of protection. This law predated the Patriot Act, and it exists largely unchanged under the Patriot Act.

Broadly speaking, electronic surveillance law makes a distinction between "content" and "envelope" information. Think of a letter you send in the mail. The content information is the letter itself. The envelope information contains the address of the recipient and your return address. The law protects content information a lot but it protects envelope information only a little.

The content-envelope distinction is based on a ruling by the U.S. Supreme Court that a list of the phone numbers a person dials (envelope information) isn't protected by the Fourth Amendment.[5] What's said during the call (content information), however, is protected. Seizing upon this distinction, Congress embodied it in the law. Content information is regulated by the Wiretap Act and the Stored Communication Act, and it is given high-level privacy protection. Envelope information is protected by the Pen Register Act, which provides low-level privacy protection.[6]

What's the difference between high- versus low-level protection? Quite a lot. The Wiretap Act requires a warrant supported by probable cause, which is the same thing the Fourth Amendment requires. It also requires even more—the government must prove that alternatives to electronic surveillance won't be effective. There are more requirements as well.[7] In contrast, the Pen Register Act doesn't require a warrant or probable cause. All the government needs to do is certify that "the information likely to be obtained . . . is relevant to an ongoing investigation."[8] It is hard to imagine how the government could fail to make this showing. Courts don't even review the evidence to back up the government's claim and must take the government's word without question.[9]

The law wrongly protects envelope information much less than content information.[10] Envelope information can reveal a lot about a person's private activities, sometimes as much (and even more) than can content information. We may care more about keeping private *who* we're talking to than *what* we're saying. Indeed, as I discussed in Chapter 15, maintaining the privacy of the identities of the people we communicate with is an important component of freedom of association under the First Amendment. Envelope information isn't innocuous, and the privacy interests in protecting it can be just as strong as content information.

The biggest problem with the envelope-content distinction is how to square it with modern technology. Table 2 shows how the distinction works for letters and phone calls. With email, the distinction falls fairly clearly on the map. The email header, which contains the addresses of the sender and recipient, is envelope information. The body of the email message is content information.

Web browsing, however, is much more complicated.

IP Addresses

An Internet Protocol (IP) address is a unique identifier assigned to every computer attached to the Internet. It's a number, such as 86.116.230.181. Each website has an IP address. On the surface, a list of IP addresses is simply a list of numbers. This seems to be analogous to envelope information, akin to phone numbers or addresses.

But it is actually much more. With a complete listing of IP addresses, the government can learn quite a lot about you because it can trace how you surf the Internet (see Table 3). From IP addresses, the government can learn the names of stores at which you shop, the

Table 2   The Envelope-Content Distinction

Technology	Envelope	Content
Postal mail	Name and address of sender and recipient	Letter
Phone call	Phone number dialed or received	Spoken communication

political organizations you find interesting, your sexual fantasies, your health concerns, and so on. IP addresses are thus much more telling than phone numbers. Although who you call on the phone can be quite revealing, how you browse the Web exposes even more of your private life, for it reflects what you're thinking and reading.

URLs

What about uniform resource locators (URLs)? When you surf in your Web browser, the URL appears in the little box at the top of your browser. A URL points to the location of particular information on the Internet. This seems like an address. At first glance, it appears to be akin to envelope information.

Table 3   A Typical Array of IP Addresses

IP Address	Computer
92.220.180.20	Amazon.com
83.450.320.111	Your home computer
38.303.1.842	Greenpeace
29.404.60.201	Your work computer
39.40.098.202	*Star Wars* fan website
172.171.0.12	Alcoholics Anonymous
20.56.002.20	Republican National Committee

But the issue is much more complex. For example, suppose you're browsing for books on Amazon.com. You're interested in books I've written, so you go to the page for my book, *The Future of Reputation: Gossip, Rumor, and Privacy on the Internet.* Here's the URL:

http://www.amazon.com/Future-Reputation-Gossip-Privacy-Internet/
dp/0300144229/ref=pd_sim_b_1

As you can see, URLs can reveal information about the title of my book, which shows what you're looking at while Web surfing.

URLs can also contain search terms. Suppose you've got pancreatic cancer and are researching treatment options. You go to Google and type in "best hospital for treatment of pancreatic cancer."

Figure 1. A Google search

You'll be redirected to your search results, at a URL something like this:

http://www.google.com/#hl=en&source=hp&q=best+hospital+
for+treatment+of+pancreatic+cancer&aq=f&aqi=&aql=&oq=
&gs_rfai=&fp=59568d73ba32e248

If you look closely, you'll see your search terms in the URL. All searches you enter will produce URLs with your search terms.

URLs seem to be much more revealing than mere location information. They capture the substance of how a person is searching the Internet. In many circumstances, to adapt media scholar Marshall McLuhan's famous maxim, the envelope *is* the content.[11]

Envelope or Content?

Before the Patriot Act, the question as to whether IP addresses and URLs were envelope or content information was unresolved. The U.S. Supreme Court hadn't looked at the question under the Fourth Amendment. Only a few lower courts had addressed the Fourth Amendment issue. As for the statutory law, the Pen Register Act spoke explicitly in terms of phone calls. It applied only to devices that recorded "the numbers dialed . . . on the telephone line."[12]

Enter the Patriot Act. It expanded the definition to all "dialing, routing, addressing, or signaling information" beyond telephone lines to numerous forms of transmission.[13]

What does this change mean? The Patriot Act appeared to expand the Pen Register Act to include email headers, IP addresses, and URLs, since they involve "routing" and "addressing" information. In other words, the Patriot Act appeared to be declaring that email headers, IP addresses, and URLs were all envelope information (Table 4).

Privacy advocates were livid. Treating all addressing and routing data as envelope information—especially IP addresses and URLs— was placing them in a category receiving very low protection. In defense of the Patriot Act, however, the law professor Orin Kerr argued

Table 4   The Patriot Act's View of Envelope and Content Information

Technology	Envelope	Content
Postal mail	Name and address of sender and recipient	Letter
Phone call	Phone number dialed or received	Spoken communication
Email	Header (To, From, Cc)	Body of email
Web surfing	IP addresses, URLs	Website text

that expanding the Pen Register Act actually increases privacy protection.[14] If the Fourth Amendment doesn't protect email headers, IP addresses, and URLs (issues that remain unresolved by the U.S. Supreme Court), then at least the Pen Register Act provides a small amount of protection, and something is better than nothing.

On the other hand, the Patriot Act rubbed salt in an existing wound. The act tried to classify these new technologies as envelope information, thus professing a resolution to the ongoing debate about how they should be categorized.

Ironically, the Patriot Act resolved little. Also embedded in the definition of pen registers was the language (added by the Patriot Act) that the information they obtain "shall not include the contents of any communication."[15] If IP addresses and URLs contain content information, then they're not covered by the Pen Register Act. But that's the very issue that the expanded definition of a pen register was supposed to resolve! In the end, the Patriot Act just begged the question.

Section 215 of the Patriot Act and National Security Letters

One of the most criticized parts of the Patriot Act is Section 215, which states:

> The Director of the Federal Bureau of Investigation or a designee of the Director (whose rank shall be no lower than Assistant Special Agent in Charge) may make an application for an order requiring the production of any tangible things (including books, records, papers, documents, and other items) for an investigation to protect against international terrorism or clandestine intelligence activities, provided that such investigation of a United States person is not conducted solely upon the basis of activities protected by the first amendment to the Constitution.[16]

This part of the law raised considerable alarm, especially since it listed "books" and "papers." Many strongly decried Section 215.

The American Library Association mounted an extensive campaign against this provision, raising the concern that it could be used by the government to obtain a person's library records. The librarians raised such a ruckus that their campaign was dubbed the "Attack of the Angry Librarians." Congress later enacted a restriction that Section 215 not be used to obtain library records for books (but allowed it for information about computer use).[17]

Section 215 is problematic, but like much of the Patriot Act, it isn't all that new. Many similar kinds of provisions already existed in electronic-surveillance law prior to the act. Before the Patriot Act, several federal laws permitted National Security Letters (NSLs), which function very similarly to Section 215.[18] The recipient of an NSL must turn over various records and data pertaining to individuals. NSLs don't require probable cause, a warrant, or even judicial oversight. Compliance is mandatory. According to one estimate, the FBI issues about thirty thousand NSLs per year.[19] Getting rid of the Patriot Act will only eliminate Section 215; it won't get rid of NSLs.

Before the Patriot Act, the protection of library records wasn't very strong. Most state laws permitted the government to obtain library records with a mere subpoena.[20] As I've discussed, subpoenas provide hardly any protection. Certainly, Section 215 provides even less protection, but the law before Section 215 was far from sufficient.

The Symbolism of the Patriot Act

The Patriot Act has become a lightning rod for all problematic instances of government information gathering. Certainly, many provisions of the Patriot Act are problematic, but it is important to realize that the Patriot Act is a small part of a much larger body of law pertaining to government surveillance. It is necessary to understand the big picture of how electronic surveillance law works. The law had severe problems before the Patriot Act. Repealing the act won't give us back our privacy.

17

The Law-and-Technology Problem and the Leave-It-to-the-Legislature Argument

uppose the government wants to read my email messages. I'm an email packrat, saving thousands of messages I send and receive, and they paint an intricate portrait of my life. Needless to say, I prefer not to have some government official foraging through my email accounts.

The good news is that there's an extensive body of federal statutory law that regulates when and how the government can access email. Statutes are playing an increasingly important role in regulating government information gathering. Some commentators contend that statutes passed by legislatures are much better at regulating new technologies than are constitutional rights recognized by courts.

So what kind of protection do the federal statutes give me? Here's the bad news—the answer is surprisingly difficult. I can't even generalize by saying "a lot" or "a little." All I can say is "it depends." It depends upon what kind of email system I'm using. It depends upon how my email is stored. And it depends upon how courts will interpret statutes written long before email was in widespread popular use. Later on, I'll walk you through the answer just to make your head spin.

The question of what kind of privacy protection the federal statutes give to email should be an easy one to resolve. Email has become one of the most ubiquitous modes of communication today. How can there not be an easy answer?

The reason is that the law struggles in dealing with new technology. Those who favor statutes argue that legislatures do a better job than courts. But judges and legislators can be equally inept when crafting rules to deal with developing technologies. The solution isn't to say "leave it to the legislature" or "leave it to the courts" but for both legislatures and courts to cooperate in creating rules that can grow and evolve as technology develops.

In this chapter, I critique the leave-it-to-the-legislature argument and explore how we should deal with changing technology. If every rule we pass becomes obsolete a year afterward, the law will always be huffing and puffing to catch up, and it never will. Can we fix this problem? I argue that we can.

The Leave-It-to-the-Legislature Argument

Orin Kerr, a leading expert on electronic-surveillance law, contends that legislatures are better than courts at creating rules involving new technologies.[1] Kerr concludes that courts should defer to legislatures in these situations. He reasons that legislatures create more comprehensive rules than judges applying the Fourth Amendment, that statutes are clearer than Fourth Amendment law, and that legislatures are better able to keep up with technological changes than judges.[2]

Kerr is wrong on all counts. First, the statutes aren't more comprehensive than Fourth Amendment protection. Congress has failed to regulate many new technologies. Where's the regulation on global positioning systems, which can be used to track people's movements? On satellite surveillance? On radio frequency identification devices? On thermal imaging devices, which can detect movement inside buildings based on heat patterns?

Although Congress has passed laws to regulate government

access to the extensive digital dossiers about us stored in various computer systems, there are many gaps in these laws. Although at least two statutes regulate government access to financial data, there are many situations where financial data is unprotected, such as when the information is held by employers, landlords, merchants, creditors, database companies, and others.[3] The statutes focus on who is holding the information, rather than on the information itself. The same piece of information can be protected if held by one third party and completely unprotected if held by a different third party. Thus the statutory regulation of new technologies is hardly comprehensive, and where there is protection, it is riddled with holes.

Second, the statutes are just as unclear as the Fourth Amendment —perhaps even more so. Indeed, Kerr admits that federal electronic surveillance statutes are "famously complex, if not entirely impenetrable."[4] Courts have described these statutes as caught up in a "fog," "convoluted," "fraught with trip wires," and "confusing and uncertain."[5]

Third, legislatures aren't better than courts at crafting rules to deal with changing technology. According to Kerr, courts, unlike legislatures, "cannot update rules quickly as technology shifts."[6] But Congress has failed in this regard as well. During the development of the Internet, email, and the dizzying array of other new technologies throughout the past quarter-century, Congress made only a few major revisions to electronic-surveillance law. And though the invention of the telephone and the rise of wiretapping occurred in the late nineteenth century, Congress didn't regulate wiretapping until 1934. That statute quickly proved to be ineffective, and it accomplished the amazing feat of earning the scorn of privacy advocates as well as law-enforcement officials.[7] Finally, in 1968, Congress reworked the law of wiretapping, and the law regulating the telephone was at long last in decent shape.

Then came the rise of computers. The next major overhaul was in 1986, when Congress realized that computers were here to stay and needed to be included in the law of electronic surveillance. So it passed the Electronic Communications Privacy Act (ECPA). And then . . . nothing. There were some laws that made changes here and there, but the basic structure of protections for the Internet and email remained largely unchanged during the next twenty-five years. The Patriot Act of 2001 made the most significant changes, but these were more tweaks rather than a major structural overhaul.

Thus the framework for the electronic-surveillance law we have today is based on ECPA from 1986. Back then, I was using an Apple IIe computer, with a clunky monochrome monitor, a floppy disk drive, and barely enough memory to store a paper longer than twenty pages. I didn't even know about email or the Internet. Needless to say, a lot has changed since then.

If anything, the historical record suggests that Congress is actually far worse than the courts in reacting to new technologies. This history shouldn't be surprising. Indeed, it is hard to imagine Congress keeping statutes up to date. Federal legislation is not easy to pass, and it usually takes a dramatic event to spark interest in creating or updating a law. In contrast, courts must get involved every time an issue arises in a case. As a result, issues are likely to be addressed with more frequency in the courts than in Congress.

So Is My Email Protected or Not?

I opened this chapter with a question: *What kind of protection do the federal statutes provide when the government wants to read my email?* The answer is immensely complicated. There are at least three statutes that regulate email, and all are part of ECPA—the Wiretap Act, the Stored Communications Act, and the Pen Register Act. Each provides very different levels of protection.

The Wiretap Act governs communications intercepted while in transmission. A classic example is a wiretap of a phone conversation. The Wiretap Act requires the government to obtain a warrant supported by probable cause, and it has strict penalties for violations.[8] It has other restrictions too, making it even stronger than the Fourth Amendment.

The Stored Communications Act regulates communications in "electronic storage."[9] It governs law-enforcement access to subscriber records of various communications service providers, such as ISPs. It provides a medium level of protection, which in most cases isn't as strong as warrants supported by probable cause.

The Pen Register Act regulates the government's access to routing and addressing information. The act provides a very low level of protection, significantly weaker than warrants supported by probable cause.[10]

Depending upon the type of email I use, how it is stored, and how the government tries to access it, it will be covered by the Wiretap Act, various parts of the Stored Communications Act, the Pen Register Act, or none of the above.

The Wiretap Act protects against the government eavesdropping on communications while in transit. Suppose I call you on the phone, and the government taps the line and listens in. The strong protections of the Wiretap Act will regulate the government.

Now suppose I send an email to you, and the government reads it before you receive it. Does the Wiretap Act apply? Maybe. Email travels differently than do phone calls. When I send you an email, it goes to an ISP, where it sits until you download it. If the government gets it while it is traveling from my computer to the ISP, or from the ISP to your computer, then the Wiretap Act's protections will probably apply. But what if the government gets the email while it is sitting on the ISP's server, waiting for you to download it? Now it's stored, and it isn't covered by the Wiretap Act but instead is protected by the Stored Communications Act, which provides lesser protections.

What if the government wants to obtain my webmail? I access my work email messages from my Web browser rather than download them to my computer. I also have a Gmail account and Yahoo email account. I keep a lot of archived messages in these accounts long after I've read them. The Stored Communications Act protects communications in "electronic storage," so it seemingly applies.

But the answer isn't that easy. Webmail doesn't readily fit into the statutory framework designed long before most other forms of webmail existed. The Stored Communications Act categorizes computing services into two types—an "electronic communications service" (ECS) for email and a "remote computing service" (RCS) for data processing and storage. These categories get different levels of protection, with an ECS getting more protection than an RCS. I won't bore you with the definitions of these categories, but they are quite technical, and there are many debates about whether modern technologies such as cloud computing are an ECS, an RCS, or neither.

Common sense would suggest that webmail is an ECS because it is an email service and email is stored electronically. But "electronic storage" is defined as "any temporary, intermediate storage" that is "incidental" to the communication and "any storage of such communication by an electronic communications service for purpose of backup protection of such communication."[11] The language is clunky and confusing. It is clear that email sitting on the ISP's server waiting to be downloaded is in "electronic storage," which is what the drafters of the statute had in mind. The law was written in the days when people accessed their email by dialing in with a modem and downloading it to their computers. No matter how prescient, the members of Congress could not predict that a company like Google would come along and offer people free email accounts with many gigabytes of storage space. Even one gigabyte of storage would have been an extravagant luxury back in 1986, and such vast volumes being doled out faster than land in the Old West would have struck members of Congress as the stuff of science fiction.

Because messages are stored indefinitely in a person's webmail, according to the Department of Justice's interpretation, the email is no longer in temporary storage and is "simply a remotely stored file."[12] And email messages might not be stored for "backup protection" because that was meant as backup protection for ISPs, not by a person for her own personal use.[13]

Therefore, under this view, my use of webmail to archive messages doesn't fall within the definition of an ECS. Maybe it's an RCS then, subject to weaker protections, though even that isn't clear. Based on the practices back in 1986, the law says that if a provider of computer storage accesses people's content for anything except "storage or computer processing," then it is no longer an RCS. Gmail and other webmail services access people's content to deliver advertisements, so they might not be an RCS.

And there's more. Email headers—the to/from lines of my email—are regulated by a different statute—the Pen Register Act. I could go on, but I'll spare you further details. My purpose has been to demonstrate that trying to fit ever-changing technologies into antiquated rules can become confusing and counterproductive.

Solving the Law-and-Technology Problem

The law-and-technology problem can't readily be solved by favoring legislatures over courts or vice versa. The problem stems from the way legal rules are created. Laws must have sufficient breadth and flexibility to deal with rapidly evolving technology. The electronic-surveillance statutes were built too closely around existing technology at the time, a guarantee that they would become outdated as technology evolved. As a result, the degree of protection that information receives from certain forms of government information gathering often turns not on how problematic the governmental intrusion is but on legal technicalities.

Under this state of affairs, law enforcement cleverly uses new technologies to avoid triggering strong statutory privacy protections. Often these technologies are quite invasive, but the debate seems to turn on whether the surveillance fits into a framework developed decades before these technologies were created or matured into their current form.

In one case, for example, the FBI wanted to figure out the alleged mobster Nicky Scarfo's password to his computer. Agents installed a device known as a key logger system on his computer to record his keystrokes. With the keystroke-logging device, the FBI was able to figure out Scarfo's password—which turned out to be the prison number of his father, Nicky Scarfo, Sr. Scarfo argued that the keystroke logger was akin to a wiretap and therefore the Wiretap Act should apply. But the FBI was clever when it designed the device. The key logger system would record keystrokes only when Scarfo was offline. The device thus didn't capture any communication in transit.[14] This seems like an end-run around the law.

Lost amid the labyrinthine task of applying ECPA's complex provisions is the question of whether new technologies contravene the appropriate balance between effective law enforcement and privacy. Basic principles are lost in the shuffle. But principles should guide technology, not vice versa. Instead of pondering statutory puzzles, the law should focus on the real issues at stake: Does a particular technology pose a threat to privacy? What are the dangers? How might they be mitigated or controlled?

We need a surveillance law that is flexible enough to respond to emerging technologies, and to do so it must begin with basic principles. As I argued in Chapter 4, courts shouldn't defer to legislatures. Instead, as I contended in Chapter 12, courts should recognize a broad scope of Fourth Amendment protection. I referred to this as the Coverage Question, and I recommended that the Fourth Amendment should regulate whenever government information gathering caused problems of reasonable significance.

What kind of broad principles should courts derive from the Fourth Amendment? This is an issue that falls under what I call the Procedure Question, which involves the kind of oversight and regulation the Fourth Amendment should provide. I suggest at least three basic principles for regulating privacy and security:

1. *Minimize gathering and use.* The government should seek to minimize the extent to which it gathers personal information beyond what is needed for security purposes. The future uses of data must be limited so that data collected for one purpose isn't someday unexpectedly used for an unrelated purpose. And data should be deleted after a reasonable period of time.

2. *Particularized suspicion.* The government should restrict its information gathering to circumstances involving particularized suspicion. As I argued in Chapter 13, dragnet searches should be restricted.

3. *Oversight.* Government information gathering and use must be subjected to meaningful oversight. Government officials must be supervised to ensure that they keep their activities circumscribed, prevent abuses of power, and remain accountable for their behavior.

These are broad principles. The role of legislatures should be to fill in the details. Courts should be respectful of statutes if they meet the general principles of the Fourth Amendment. Courts shouldn't hold law-enforcement activity invalid simply because it wasn't conducted according to the regular Fourth Amendment rules that courts have established. Courts should accept statutory provisions that depart from judicially created Fourth Amendment rules as long as they satisfy Fourth Amendment principles. Courts shouldn't have a monopoly on crafting the rules, and this is where courts and legislatures can establish a useful dialogue.[15]

Electronic-surveillance statutes should be rewritten with a

new baseline. Currently, many forms of government information gathering involving electronic communications and surveillance fall outside statutory protection because the new technologies don't fit. The current baseline is that unless something fits, it's not protected. The baseline should be shifted to the opposite approach, one that is broad and inclusive. The law should regulate all forms of government information gathering unless specifically exempted. The starting point should be a requirement of a warrant supported by probable cause for most forms of government information gathering.[16] This should be the general rule, with specific exceptions authorizing access under less strict standards enumerated in the statute.

The key aspect of this approach is that it refocuses the debate. The discussion will be about the specific instances where warrants are too cumbersome, rather than over technicalities. As technology continues to develop, the burden should be on law-enforcement officials to convince Congress that a new device doesn't threaten privacy and that they should be authorized to use it without obtaining a warrant. The problem with the current law is that the FBI can try out new technologies in secret. Unless these technologies are reported to the public, which sometimes sparks an outcry, there will be little pressure on Congress to investigate them and determine whether to enact protections. Placing the burden on law enforcement to lobby Congress to use new technology would ensure necessary debate and discussion about the costs and benefits of these technologies.

What makes this simple approach preferable is that it is more adaptable to changing technology than the highly technical provisions of much of current wiretap law. It allows law enforcement to engage in surveillance while keeping it circumscribed and accountable.

18

Video Surveillance and the No-Privacy-in-Public Argument

In the 1998 movie *Enemy of the State*, Will Smith plays an unwitting recipient of evidence of a crime by a corrupt National Security Agency official. He is placed under ruthless surveillance, caught everywhere on camera, watched by satellites, tracked by homing devices. Far from the stuff of hyperactive Hollywood imagination, much of the surveillance technology in the movie is fact, not fiction.

Across the pond in the United Kingdom, more than four million surveillance cameras stand guard over nearly every square inch of London, as well as other metropolitan areas. Begun in 1994 in response to a series of terrorist bombings, the surveillance system consists of video cameras monitored by officials via closed-circuit television—called CCTV.[1]

Can such a system be implemented in the United States? "We've got a Constitution," one might say, "and the U.K. doesn't. The government can't do that kind of thing in America."

But this is wrong. The government *can* do it and *is* doing it. Unlike the centralized system in the United Kingdom, the surveillance in the United States is more fragmented. But it is growing. Government surveillance cameras are being installed in public places all the time. Washington, D.C., now has more than forty-eight hundred government surveillance cameras, and Chicago has seven hundred. In 2006 a report indicated that 25 percent of U.S. cities were investing in surveillance camera systems, and since then the number has continued to increase.[2]

Will the Fourth Amendment regulate it? What about all the electronic-surveillance statutes? The answer is no. Public video surveillance falls outside the protection of the Fourth Amendment and electronic-surveillance law. In this chapter, I argue that public video surveillance should be regulated.

Why Doesn't the Law Regulate Public Video Surveillance?

Listening vs. Watching

Suppose you're sitting outside at a café chatting with your friend. The government installs a bugging device and records your conversation. Do the electronic-surveillance statutes provide protection?

Yes. The Wiretap Act will protect you from clandestine bugging. It kicks in when you have an expectation that you're not being secretly bugged or recorded.[3] The fact that you're out in public and a few others can overhear you doesn't matter—you're still protected.

Now suppose the government sets up a hidden camera from a van parked on the curb next to the tables. Clever government officials record you and your friend on video, then hire a skilled lip-reader to decipher the conversation. Are you protected by the Wiretap Act?

This time, you're out of luck. Silent video surveillance is not covered under the Wiretap Act's bugging protections because it doesn't involve a human voice.[4] So you're not protected—unless you're a foreign spy. Then the government needs a court order to place you under surveillance. Ironically, the Foreign Intelligence Surveillance Act (FISA) regulates video surveillance of foreign agents. The government must submit "a detailed description of the nature of the information sought and the type of communications or activities to be subjected to the surveillance." Moreover, the government must certify "that such information cannot reasonably be obtained by normal investigative techniques."[5] Foreign agents therefore receive protection against silent video surveillance, but U.S. citizens don't.

The electronic-surveillance statutes strongly protect against the government's eavesdropping on your conversations but don't protect against the government's watching you. This distinction doesn't make a lot of sense. Video surveillance involves similar threats to privacy as audio surveillance. As one court noted: "Television surveillance is identical *in its indiscriminate character* to wiretapping and bugging. It is even more invasive of privacy, just as a strip search is more invasive than a pat-down search, but it is not more indiscriminate: the microphone is as 'dumb' as the television camera; both devices pick up anything within their electronic reach, however irrelevant to the investigation."[6]

As another court observed, "video surveillance can be vastly more intrusive [than audio surveillance], as demonstrated by the surveillance in this case that recorded a person masturbating before the hidden camera."[7]

The reason the law protects listening instead of watching is that Congress often crafts laws narrowly. When it passed the Wiretap Act in 1968, Congress didn't think of regulating surveillance in all its forms—it focused on audio surveillance, such as bugging and wiretapping. In 1986, when it revised the law with the Electronic Communication Privacy Act, it expanded its scope to email. Congress was focusing on protecting communications, not on regulating surveillance in all its forms.

The Secrecy Paradigm

Suppose you're in public and the government records your activities with a surveillance camera. Does the Fourth Amendment protect you?

No. The Fourth Amendment protects you only when you have a reasonable expectation of privacy, and the Supreme Court has held that when you can be overheard in public, you can't expect privacy.

The current Fourth Amendment law of video surveillance distinguishes between surveillance in private places and surveillance in public places. Surveillance in private places is protected, but surveillance in public places is not. The law has a particular view of privacy, one I called the "secrecy paradigm" in Chapter 10. The law is obsessed with secrecy—if something occurs in secret, hidden away from others, concealed from the world, then it is considered "private" and given legal protection. If something is exposed to others or done in public, then it's no longer secret and isn't given legal protection.

The law seems to have in mind the frightening world of George Orwell's Big Brother, where all people had telescreens installed in their homes. As people watched TV, the government could watch them.[8] The Fourth Amendment will protect you against the government installing a telescreen in your house, so you're safe from Orwellian dystopia. But it won't protect you beyond the small zone in which you live in secrecy.

To illustrate how potent the secrecy paradigm is, suppose the government launches a new satellite and surveillance camera system that can track and record all citizens' activities in public throughout their lifetimes. Any Fourth Amendment protection?

No. In *California v. Ciraolo*, the Court held that while in public, people lack a reasonable expectation of privacy from visual observation from above.[9] The government could record everything you do in public from your birth to death, and the Fourth Amendment would be completely inapplicable. Indeed, the government could continuously record everything all three hundred million citizens do in public, and the Fourth Amendment would provide no protection.

So here's where the law stands. The Fourth Amendment

will provide you with protection only when you're at home or in a private place. If you're in park or at a store or restaurant, you have no Fourth Amendment protection from video surveillance. The electronic-surveillance statutes will protect you only if you're a foreign spy.

Regulating Surveillance

Abandoning the Secrecy Paradigm

Should we have more protection against public video surveil-lance? Many argue that people shouldn't expect privacy in public. "If you're out in the open, how can you possibly expect to be private?" one might ask.

This is the logic of the secrecy paradigm. The problem with the secrecy paradigm is that we *do* expect some degree of privacy in pub-lic. We don't expect total secrecy, but we also don't expect somebody to be recording everything we do. Most of the time, when we're out and about, nobody's paying any special attention to us. We do many private things in public, such as buy medications and hygiene prod-ucts in drug stores and browse books and magazines in bookstores. We expect a kind of practical obscurity—to be just another face in the crowd.[10]

Video surveillance is problematic regardless of whether it oc-curs in private or in public. Even in public places, surveillance can lead to self-censorship and inhibition.[11] As the legal scholar Julie Cohen puts it, "Pervasive monitoring of every first move or false start will, at the margin, incline choices toward the bland and the main-stream."[12]

Surveillance limits our freedom. It can tie us to our past by creating a trail of information about us. It can make it difficult for us to speak anonymously. It can make our behavior less spontaneous and make us more self-conscious about where we go and what we do.[13]

Surveillance's inhibitory effects are especially potent when people are engaging in political protest or dissent. People can face persecution, public sanction, and blacklisting for their unpopular political beliefs. Surveillance can make associating with disfavored groups and causes all the more difficult and precarious.

Surveillance is a sweeping form of investigatory power. It extends beyond a search, for it records behavior, social interaction, and everything that a person says and does. Rather than a targeted query for information, surveillance is often akin to a dragnet search, which can ensnare a significant amount of data beyond that which was originally sought. Moreover, unlike a typical search, which is often performed in a once-and-done fashion, electronic surveillance goes on continuously.

Surveillance gives significant power to the watchers. Part of the harm is not simply in being watched but in the lack of control that people have over the watchers. Surveillance creates the need to worry about the judgment of the watchers. Will our confidential information be revealed? What will be done with the information gleaned from surveillance?

The government could develop a repository of information about citizens and then use any instances of infraction as a pretext to target people for their words or for their political beliefs and activities. The government could also use any embarrassing information it obtained from the surveillance to blackmail people. Government officials could leak such information either through carelessness or intentionally as a way to smear or otherwise retaliate against a person. In one case in the United Kingdom, a person was caught on CCTV attempting suicide by slitting his wrists. The attempt was foiled. The footage was given to a TV show called *Crime Beat*, which broadcast the incident without obscuring the subject's face.[14]

All of these problems occur with surveillance regardless of whether it occurs in public or private. When figuring out whether to regulate something, I believe it is best to begin by looking at the problems and then crafting regulation to address them. Instead of blindly following the secrecy paradigm or other theories of privacy, we should first ask: *Are there any problems?* If the answer is yes, then we should ask further: *What can the law do to fix or minimize these problems?*

Whether in public or in private, government surveillance can chill speech, dissent, and association; it provides great power to the watchers; it can be abused. The law should face these problems and get to work on fixing them.

Watching the Watchers

Defenders of surveillance cameras argue that they deter crime. But studies show that the cameras don't have particularly good success. For example, a study of sixty-eight surveillance cameras in Berkeley, California, demonstrated a decrease in property crimes near the cameras. Violent crimes also decreased near the cameras but increased away from them, suggesting that the cameras just shifted the crime geographically rather than eliminating it.[15] A study done of the United Kingdom's CCTV system indicates that the cameras had "no overall effect on all relevant crime viewed collectively."[16] The study, which was commissioned by the government, also found that the cameras failed to reduce people's fear of being victimized by crime.

When people attack surveillance cameras for failing to deter crime, defenders often respond that they're useful in solving crime. Indeed, CCTV cameras caught the London subway bombers on video. On television news shows and on crime shows, we often see surveillance camera footage of criminals caught in the act. Debates about surveillance cameras typically pit the benefits of the cameras against privacy concerns.

But this is an example of the all-or-nothing fallacy I refuted in Chapter 3. Regulating surveillance doesn't mean abolishing it. There's a famous saying about surveillance: "Who will watch the watchers?" We must ensure that those engaging in surveillance are regulated and accountable.

Therefore, I recommend the following guidelines for video surveillance:

1. *Accountability and transparency.* All video surveillance should be subjected to oversight and review. Data should be kept about the performance and effectiveness of the surveillance, as well as of any abuses and problems.
2. *Strong penalties for abuses.* Any leaks or misuses of video surveillance information should be subject to strong penalties.
3. *Deletion of old data.* Video surveillance data shouldn't be maintained indefinitely. It should be deleted after a period of time. This prevents future misuse.
4. *Prevention of mission creep.* "Mission creep" refers to the phenomenon of a task's growing beyond its original parameters. In the case of video surveillance, it means data collected for one purpose coming to be used for other purposes, or technologies installed for one purpose later being used for another. The purposes of surveillance should be specified in advance, and data collected via surveillance should be used only for those purposes. Any new uses of the data must be approved by a court, and only after the government demonstrates that the benefits of the uses outweigh any harms to privacy and civil liberties.
5. *Protection of First Amendment rights.* Video surveillance data involving speech, protest, political association, religion, and the exploration of ideas and knowledge should be subject to the most stringent of protections. The government must avoid using this data except under the most compelling circumstances.

19

Should the Government Engage in Data Mining?

I like to shop on Amazon.com. Every time I visit Amazon.com, they say to me: "Welcome, Daniel." They know me by name! And then they say: "We've got recommendations for you." I love their recommendations. They suggest various books and products I might like, and they're pretty good at it.

Amazon.com's recommendations are the product of a form of "data mining." Data mining involves creating profiles by amassing personal data and then analyzing it for nuggets of wisdom about individuals. Amazon looks at my buying pattern and compares it to similar patterns of other people. If I bought a *Lord of the Rings* movie, it might recommend a *Harry Potter* movie. Why? Because a high percentage of people buying a *Lord of the Rings* movie also bought a *Harry Potter* movie. Despite our desire to be authentic and unique, we're often similar to other people, and we're frequently quite predictable.

Some government officials think that if data mining works so well for Amazon and other companies, then it might work well for law enforcement. If data mining can predict whether I'm likely to buy a *Harry Potter* movie, maybe it can also predict whether I'm likely to commit a crime or engage in terrorism.

Generally, law enforcement is investigative, focusing on apprehending perpetrators of past crimes. When it comes to terrorism, law enforcement shifts to being more preventative, seeking to identify terrorists before they act. This is why the government has become interested in data mining—to predict who might conduct a future terrorist attack.

Proponents of data mining argue that examining information for patterns will greatly assist in locating terrorists because certain characteristics and behaviors are likely to be associated with terrorist activity. As Judge Richard Posner argues, in "an era of global terrorism and proliferation of weapons of mass destruction, the government has a compelling need to gather, pool, sift, and search vast quantities of information, much of it personal."[1]

Data mining supporters contend that because it involves computers analyzing data, the information is rarely seen by humans, so there's no privacy harm. They also argue that there's no privacy harm because much of the data already exists in databases, so nothing new is being disclosed. And as the law professor Eric Goldman argues, in many cases people don't even know their data is being analyzed. He declares: "This situation brings to mind the ancient Zen parable: if a tree falls in a forest and no one is around to hear it, does it make a sound?"[2]

Should the government engage in data mining? In this chapter, I'll explain when it should and when it shouldn't.

The Rise of Government Data Mining

In 2002 the Department of Defense, under the guidance of Admiral John Poindexter, began developing a data mining project called Total Information Awareness (TIA). Under the TIA program, the government planned to assemble a massive database consisting of financial, educational, health, and other information on U.S. citizens, which would later be analyzed to single out people matching a terrorist pro-

Figure 2. The (defunct) TIA logo

file. According to Poindexter, terrorists can be caught by looking at "patterns of activity that are based on observations from past terrorist attacks."[3]

The TIA program had its own website, with a slick logo (Figure 2). At the top of the pyramid was an eye, with beams of light emanating from it and illuminating the globe. Toward the bottom, in Latin, was the motto: "Knowledge is power."

Media reports about the program sparked a public outcry. The late William Safire, then a conservative columnist for the *New York Times,* led the charge. He declared that Poindexter "is determined to break down the wall between commercial snooping and secret government intrusion. . . . And he has been given a $200 million budget to create computer dossiers on 300 million Americans."[4]

Caught in the headlights, the Department of Defense quickly dropped the logo, changed the name of the program to Terrorism Information Awareness, and promised to protect privacy. But it was too late. Outrage about the program reached such a fever pitch that the Senate voted unanimously to deny it funding. TIA had been slain.[5]

But TIA didn't really die. Instead, it lived on in various projects with obscure names such as Basketball, Genoa II, and Topsail. Unlike TIA, which had its own website, these projects are significantly more clandestine.[6]

What lesson did the government learn from the public outrage at TIA? Did it learn that engaging in a massive data mining project raises substantial public concerns and shouldn't be done without adequate oversight, limitation, and protection of privacy? No. Instead, it learned to keep the data mining projects more hidden, to name them more innocuously, and not to have a website or a totalitarian logo.

Beyond TIA and its spin-offs, the government has been developing other data mining programs. One government report noted that "TIA was not the tip of the iceberg, but rather one small specimen in a sea of icebergs."[7] Following the September 11 attacks, the Transportation Security Administration, with the help of the FBI, has been developing a program to mine data about airline passengers to determine who should be allowed to fly, selected for extra screening, or denied the right to board an aircraft. Countless other data mining programs are being used or developed—about two hundred according to one report.[8]

The Problems of Data Mining

Defenders of data mining insist that it causes only minimal privacy harms. As Richard Posner argues:

> The collection, mainly through electronic means, of vast amounts of personal data is said to invade privacy. But machine collection and processing of data cannot, as such, invade privacy. Because of their volume, the data are first sifted by computers, which search for names, addresses, phone numbers, etc., that may have intelligence value. This initial sifting, far from invading privacy (a computer is not a sentient being), keeps most private data from being read by any intelligence officer.[9]

The potential harm from data mining, according to Posner, is use of the information to blackmail an "administration's critics and political opponents" or to "ridicule or embarrass."[10] This argument defines the privacy problems with data mining in narrow ways that neglect to account for the full panoply of problems created by the practice. Posner focuses on the problems of disclosure and the threat of disclosure (blackmail). But data mining involves many other kinds of problems, which I'll now discuss.

Inaccuracy

Data mining isn't very accurate in the behavioral predictions it makes. The difficulty is that while patterns repeat themselves, they don't do so with perfect regularity. We can be fairly confident in predicting that gravity will still work tomorrow. But predicting the weather isn't as easy—and certainly, human behavior is far more unpredictable than the weather.

Consider the following profiles:

1. "John" was a young man who was born and raised in Egypt. His parents were Muslim, though not strongly religious. His father was a successful attorney and his mother came from a wealthy family. He had two sisters, one of whom became a doctor, the other a professor. John studied architecture at Cairo University. He later lived in Germany and worked at an urban-planning firm. He had a number of close friends, and he lived with roommates. He increasingly became more religious, eventually founding a prayer group. After five years in Germany, he came to the United States. He decided to enroll in flying school to learn how to fly airplanes.[11]

2. "Matt" was a young man who was born and raised near Buffalo, New York. His parents were Catholic, but Matt later became an

agnostic. He had two sisters. His parents were middle class, and his father worked at a General Motors factory. He was a good student in high school, but he dropped out of college. He liked to collect guns, and he strongly believed in gun rights. Matt enjoyed computer programming. He enlisted in the U.S. Army. After leaving the army, he worked as a security guard. He maintained close ties with several friends he met in the army.[12]

3. "Bill" was a middle-aged man born in Chicago to middle-class parents. He was admitted at an early age to Harvard. He received a Ph.D. in math from Michigan, and then became a professor at Berkeley. He later quit the professorship and moved to a cabin in the woods. He enjoyed reading history books, riding his bike, and gardening.[13]

"John" is Mohammed Atta, the ringleader of the September 11 attacks. "Matt" is Timothy McVeigh, who bombed the Alfred P. Murrah Federal Building in Oklahoma City in 1995, killing 168 people. "Bill" is Theodore Kaczynski, the Unabomber, who mailed bombs to people for a period of nearly twenty years. These three individuals had very different backgrounds and beliefs. Atta had radicalized Islamic beliefs, McVeigh was an agnostic who believed the power of the U.S. government was running amok, and Kaczynski was an atheist who hated modern technology and industry.

Terrorists come not in just one flavor but in many, making it more difficult to construct an accurate profile. Atta, McVeigh, and Kaczynski had vastly different political beliefs, childhoods, families, socioeconomic backgrounds, levels of intelligence, and religions. Interestingly, all came from apparently normal families. Many other individuals have similar backgrounds, similar religious and political beliefs, and similar behavior patterns, but no desire to commit terrorist acts.

The things terrorists of the future do may be similar to the things done by terrorists of the past, but they also may be different. By focusing on patterns based on past experience, we may ignore new characteristics and behaviors of the terrorists of the future.[14]

Data mining proponents might reply that although not all terrorists repeat the past, they nonetheless might have some things in common, so looking at behavior patterns might still help us identify them. The problem is that even if data mining identifies some terrorists correctly, it is effective only if it doesn't have too many "false positives" — people who fit the profile but who aren't terrorists.

More than two million people fly each day worldwide.[15] A data mining program to identify terrorists with a false positive rate of 1 percent (which would be exceptionally low for such a program) would flag more than twenty thousand false positives every day. This is quite a large number of innocent people who will be wrongly snagged by the system.[16]

Why is the government so interested in data mining when the accuracy and workability of the practice remain uncertain? Part of the government's interest in data mining stems from the aggressive marketing efforts of database companies. After September 11, database companies met with government officials and made a persuasive pitch about the virtues of data mining.[17] The technology, which often works quite well in the commercial setting, can sound dazzling when presented by skillful marketers.

The problem, however, is that just because data mining might be effective for businesses trying to predict customer behavior, it isn't necessarily effective for government officials trying to predict who will engage in terrorism. A high level of accuracy is not essential when data mining is used by businesses to target marketing for consumers, because the cost of error to individuals is minimal. If Amazon.com makes a poor book recommendation to me, there's little harm. I just move on to the next recommendation. But the consequences of government data mining are vastly greater: being singled out for extra investigation, repeatedly being subjected to extra screening at the airport, being stranded while on a no-fly list, or even being arrested.

First Amendment Concerns

Another potential threat posed by data mining is that it can target people based on their First Amendment–protected activities, an issue I discussed in Chapter 15. Suspicious profiles might involve information about people's free speech, free association, or religious activity. Singling people out for extra investigation, for denial of the right to travel by plane, or for inclusion in a suspicious-persons blacklist is more troubling if the action is based even in part on protected First Amendment activities. How do we know that the profiles aren't based on a person's free expression? What if a person is singled out for extra investigation based on his unpopular political views? How do we know that the profiles aren't based upon a person's religious activity? If people are members of unpopular political groups, do they get singled out for extra screening at the airport?

Information gathering about First Amendment–protected activities involving people's reading habits and speech might chill the exercise of these rights. There doesn't need to be a leak to deter people from reading unpopular books or saying unpopular things. People might be deterred by the fact that the government can readily learn about what a person reads and says—and that the government might mine this data to make predictions about a person's behavior.

Suppose I perform the following searches on Google about ricin, a poison made from castor beans that can be lethal if ingested or inhaled:

obtain ricin
where to buy castor beans

lethal dosage of ricin

how to administer ricin

how to make ricin from castor beans

Suppose I also buy a book on Amazon called *The Idiot's Guide to Using Poison*. Looks quite suspicious, doesn't it? But I have an innocent explanation: I'm writing a novel about a character who murders someone with ricin. Although I have no intent to do evil, I certainly wouldn't want some nervous government law-enforcement officials to see my activities. Nor would I want some computer to start beeping because of my odd buying and Web-surfing behavior. Even though there's an innocent explanation, I shouldn't have to worry about explaining myself or being subjected to an investigation or extra scrutiny at the airport.

Perhaps I might be undeterred and still do the searches and buy the book. But not everyone would feel as comfortable. Some people might refrain from researching ricin or other things because of a fear of potential consequences, and that's a problem in a society that values robust freedom to speak, write, and read.

Equality

Data mining also implicates the principle that people should be treated equally under the law regardless of their race, ethnicity, or religion. How do we know the extent to which race or ethnicity is used in the profiles?

Some argue that data mining helps to eliminate stereotyping and discrimination. Computers can minimize the human element, thus preventing bias and racism from entering into the process.[18] Whereas some data mining techniques involve a human-created profile of a terrorist and seek to identify people who match the profile, other data mining techniques ostensibly let the computer compose the profile by analyzing patterns of behavior from known terrorists. Even this technique, however, involves human judgment. Somebody has to make the initial judgment about who qualifies as a known terrorist and who does not. Profiles can contain pernicious assumptions hidden in the architecture of computer code and embedded in algorithms so that they appear to be the decision of neutral computers.

On the other hand, one might argue, profiling via data mining might be better than the alternatives. The legal scholar Frederick Schauer aptly notes that there is no escape from profiling, for without data mining, officials will be making their own subjective judgments about who is suspicious. These judgments are based on an implicit profile, though one that isn't overt and articulated. "[T]he issue is not about whether to use profiles or not but instead about whether to use (or to prefer) formal written profiles or informal unwritten ones."[19] Although it is true that formal profiles constructed in advance have their virtues over discretionary profiling by officials, formal profiles contain some disadvantages. They are more systematic than the discretionary approach, thus compounding the effects of information tied to race, ethnicity, religion, speech, or other factors that might be problematic. Those profiling informally are subject to scrutiny, as they have to answer in court about why they believed a person was suspicious. Data mining, however, lacks such transparency, a problem I will discuss later. Formal written profiles cease to have an advantage over informal unwritten ones if they remain hidden and unsupervised.

Due Process

Data mining also raises due-process issues. As Daniel Steinbock notes, "The most striking aspect of virtually all antiterrorist data matching and data mining decisions is the total absence of even the most rudimentary procedures for notice, hearing, or other opportunities for meaningful participation before, or even after, the deprivation [of liberty] is imposed."[20] Will those singled out by data mining programs be able to raise a challenge? Will people have a right to hearings? How long will it take for people to get hearings? Will people have a right to attorneys? Will people get to correct false data? How?

Suppose you disagree with a profile that repeatedly flags you as suspicious. You want the government to reexamine the profile. You want the opportunity to be heard. Will you get a hearing? Probably not, as the profiles are secret. Data mining proponents argue that if the profiles are revealed to the public, then the terrorists will be better able to take steps to evade them.

But what kind of meaningful challenge can you make if you're not told about the profile that you supposedly matched? How can our society evaluate the profiling systems if we are kept in the dark?

Predictive determinations about one's future behavior are much more difficult to contest than investigative determinations about one's past behavior. Wrongful investigative determinations can be addressed in adjudication. But wrongful predictions about whether a person might engage in terrorism in the future are not often ripe for judicial review. Nevertheless, people may experience negative consequences from such predictive judgments, such as being denied the ability to travel or being subject to extra scrutiny.

Imagine trying to refute a predictive judgment made about you:

DATA MINER: Your pattern of behavior indicates that you might engage in terrorism in the future.

YOU: I'm innocent.

DATA MINER: You just haven't done anything yet.

YOU: So it doesn't matter that I'm innocent?

DATA MINER: Just because you haven't done so now doesn't meant you won't do so in the future.

YOU: How do I prove that I won't do something I haven't done yet?

DATA MINER: You can't. That's why we want to watch you for the rest of your life.

YOU: Why do you think I'm going to commit terrorism in the future?

DATA MINER: We can't tell you that. Then you would change your behavior and we couldn't detect future terrorists like you.

YOU: But I'm not going to be a terrorist.

DATA MINER: Only because we'll be keeping you under extra scrutiny.

In the real world, you'd never have this conversation, because you'd never be privy to any details about the data mining. Earlier I mentioned the resemblance between some privacy problems and the dystopia of Franz Kafka's *The Trial.* Kafka wrote about a hapless man who was arrested but never told the reason why. The man became obsessed with finding out more, including what was going to happen to him and how he could prove his innocence. Despite his efforts, he could never find out the charges against him, let alone refute them. Data mining can throw people into the same kind of bureaucratic morass—they are deemed suspicious but can't find out why and so can do nothing to refute the suspicion.

Transparency

The key problem with data mining is that it is hard to carry out with transparency. Transparency, or openness, is essential to promote accountability and to provide the public with a way to ensure that government officials are not engaging in abuse. "Sunlight is said to be the best of disinfectants," Justice Brandeis declared, "electric light the most efficient policeman."[21] As James Madison stated: "A popular government without popular information or the means of acquiring it is but a prologue to a farce or a tragedy or perhaps both. Knowledge will forever govern ignorance. And a people who mean to be their own governors must arm themselves with the power which knowledge gives."[22]

One problem with many data mining programs is that they lack adequate transparency. The programs are secret because revealing the patterns that trigger identification as a possible future terrorist will tip off terrorists about what behaviors to avoid. This is indeed a legitimate concern. Our society, however, is one of open government, public accountability, and oversight of government officials—not one of secret blacklists maintained by bureaucracies. Without public accountability, unelected bureaucrats can administer data mining programs in ways often insulated from any scrutiny at all. For example, the information gathered about people for use in data mining might be collected from sources that don't take sufficient steps to maintain accuracy. Without oversight, it is unclear what level of accuracy the government requires for the information it gathers and uses. If profiles are secretly based on race, speech, or other factors that society might find troublesome to rely upon, how can this fact ever be aired and discussed? If a person is routinely singled out based on a profile and wants to challenge the profile, there appears to be no way to do so unless the profile is revealed.

The lack of transparency in data mining programs makes it nearly impossible to balance the privacy and security interests. Given the significant potential privacy issues and other constitutional concerns, combined with speculative and unproven security benefits as well as the availability of many other alternative means of promoting security, should data mining still be on the table as a viable policy option? One could argue that data mining at least should be investigated and studied. There is nothing wrong with doing so, but the cost must be considered in light of alternative security measures that might already be effective and present fewer potential problems.

When Should the Government Be Permitted to Engage in Data Mining?

As you can probably deduce, I'm not a big fan of data mining when it is done by the government. I don't reject all government data mining. In particular, I support government data mining when there's a specific threat and specific information about the likely perpetrators. I don't support data mining when it is done to make general behavioral predictions. When data mining is done in this general predictive way, it is essentially a dragnet search—casting a giant net to see what it brings in. In many ways, this practice resembles general warrants, the broad fishing expeditions for criminal activity that the Framers of the Constitution wanted to curtail when creating the Fourth Amendment.

To make things more concrete, consider the following hypothetical situations:

The Ticking Bomb

Suppose the FBI receives a tip from a credible source that two young males, both naturalized U.S. citizens, who are Muslim and who were born in Saudi Arabia, have rented a U-Haul truck and are planning to use it to detonate a bomb tomorrow at a building in Los Angeles. The source says that he met the two males at his mosque, which has more than one thousand worshipers. This is all the information the FBI agents have. Agents scramble to investigate.

The FBI seeks the records of the people who attend the mosque and the records of U-Haul. The FBI wants to cross-reference these two sets of records to identify any male member of the mosque who rented a U-Haul. Should the FBI be able to obtain the records?

Yes. I support this form of data mining, so long as it is conducted with adequate judicial oversight. I support it because the data mining begins based not on a hunch, not on some abstract profile, but on a tip that points to specific information about a specific attack. Given the time pressures and the need for more information, comparing the records will help pinpoint the identities of the potential attackers. The justification to see the records is far from speculative.

I would require strong judicial oversight. I'd require the government to explain the nature of the tip to a court (to ensure that the tip is legitimate). Because the records of the mosque implicate freedom of religion, I'd be extremely careful in allowing the government to use them. I'd first require the government to show why the U-Haul records alone won't be sufficient to narrow down their investigation. I'd also require the government to destroy the records after using them.

Suspicious Flight Students

Suppose a recent terrorist had attended flight school and was of Middle Eastern ethnicity. The government wants to single out all people who match this profile for further investigation.

This is a form of predictive data mining, and I believe its costs outweigh its benefits. Unlike the ticking bomb scenario, there is no specific threat. The government is just on the hunt for people it thinks are suspicious. There isn't a tip or any other evidence to suggest that the particular pattern of behavior is connected to future terrorist plotting. The fact that prior terrorists went to flight school is not sufficient to justify a profile that flags everybody of a particular ethnicity with the ambition to be a pilot.

Airline Passenger Screening

Suppose the government develops a profile of a likely terrorist that it uses to determine who should be subjected to extra screening at the airport or denied the opportunity to fly.

I would restrict this form of data mining. The profile is likely to be too speculative, and there are no guarantees that the profiles don't single out people based on race, ethnicity, speech, religion, or other factors. There is not sufficient transparency. Nor are there protections to ensure accuracy or to afford people due process when they are systematically singled out for extra screening or not allowed to fly.

"But isn't it silly for the screeners to search grandma?" one might ask. "We all know the terrorists are young Middle Eastern males. Let's search them instead."

While it is true that in the past many terrorists have been young Middle Eastern males, this hasn't always been the case. Females as well as non–Middle Eastern people have engaged in terrorism.

Is it likely that grandma is a terrorist? No. But the odds are incredibly low that any one person is a terrorist. Finding a terrorist among the millions who travel each day is like finding a needle in a haystack. An individual fitting a profile may be statistically likelier to be a terrorist than someone who doesn't fit it, but the chances are still very small. Thus the costs associated with data mining outweigh the relatively slight chance that it will detect a terrorist. People shouldn't be systematically treated worse than other people for factors they have no power to change. A traveler shouldn't have to spend hours longer at the airport than other people just because he is a young male of Middle Eastern descent. He shouldn't have to miss flight connections. He shouldn't have to be constantly patted down. His flying shouldn't be made more onerous and less dignified than that of other people just because of his ethnicity or other characteristics. If the profile is based on his behavior, then he shouldn't have to refrain from doing things he's legally entitled to do. He shouldn't have to answer to government officials for who he is or what he does. Otherwise, he's being treated no longer as an equal but as someone who is inherently suspicious. No law-abiding citizen should be treated this way.

Skepticism about Data Mining

The government is currently seduced by data mining. It is not clear, however, that data mining warrants the attention and resources it currently receives. When we balance privacy and security, the goal should be to select the most effective security measures and to ensure they are properly regulated and overseen. The case hasn't been made that data mining is effective. Adequate ways to regulate and oversee it haven't been proposed. Its lack of transparency serves as a major impediment to any meaningful balancing of its security benefits and privacy costs.

One day, data mining might become an effective security tool. But for now, proponents of data mining must justify how its problems can be addressed and why it is better than alternative, less troublesome security measures. They haven't done so thus far.

20

The Luddite Argument, the *Titanic* Phenomenon, and the Fix-a-Problem Strategy

There's a major push going on to improve the accuracy of identification. New technologies of biometric identification are being developed and promoted, based on physical characteristics such as DNA, voice, and eye patterns. Once biometric identification is perfected, supporters argue, people will no longer be able to engage in fraud and pretend to be people they aren't.

When one points out privacy concerns, proponents reply that we should embrace new technology, not resist it like Luddites. But in many contexts, those who rush to embrace new technologies fail to heed what I call the "*Titanic* Phenomenon." The designers of the *Titanic* had such hubris, such dead certainty of its unsinkability, that they didn't provide enough lifeboats. While many new security proposals have great upsides, proponents are not giving adequate thought to the consequences if they fail. These consequences can prove catastrophic.

In this chapter, I'll explain the paradox at the core of the *Titanic* Phenomenon—the very things that make new technologies preferable to older ones ironically become their greatest liabilities. We shouldn't resist new technology, but we must be more cautious in how we implement it.

The Promise and Perils of Biometric Identification

For quite a long time, politicians have been concerned about how easy it is to obtain a fraudulent driver's license or to otherwise spoof identity. In 2005, in an effort to provide greater security from terrorism, Congress passed the Real ID Act, requiring states to demand more verification documents before issuing driver's licenses.[1] The act has proven costly for states, resulting in considerable backlash.

Proposals for improved identification keep popping up, a recent example being a proposal by Senators Charles Schumer and Lindsey Graham. Under their proposal, all U.S. citizens and legal immigrants would have to possess a special biometric identification card to obtain jobs. These cards would be issued by regional Social Security offices. The cards would be "tamper proof."[2]

Biometric identification promises more accurate security. Technology exists to identify people based on various immutable bodily features and characteristics, such as one's retina pattern, gait, facial features, and even body odor. The idea of using biometrics began with a French police official named Alphonse Bertillon, who in 1883 developed a system of identification based on bodily measurements such as the length of one's feet, the shape of one's head, tattoos, and scars.[3] The most common form of biometric identification today remains the fingerprint. Since each person's fingerprint is unique, states Michael Chertoff, the former secretary of the Department of Homeland Security, fingerprints "make ideal identifiers or ways we can separate real people from impersonators. Simply stated, fingerprints do not lie."[4]

Proponents of biometric technology argue that we shouldn't let terrorists get fake IDs. They argue that our identification system is in the Stone Age and that we need to modernize it with new technology. According to the sociologist Amitai Etzioni, "If individuals could be properly identified, public safety would be significantly enhanced and economic costs would be reduced significantly."[5] Because it allows us to be identified by our body parts, biometric identification might obviate the need to carry around a card or identification document. We can just look into an eye scanner or touch a pad.

Privacy advocates argue that a national identification system will give the government too much power. Historically, national identification systems have been used for pernicious purposes, such as rounding up people for genocide. An identification system can readily become a tool for greater government surveillance and can be used to track people's movement.[6]

I'm sympathetic to some of these arguments, but the point I want to make about the *Titanic* Phenomenon addresses what I call the "Luddite argument." This is the argument made by many security proponents that those opposed to new security technologies are Luddites, a term originally used for a group who protested the mechanization of the Industrial Revolution in the nineteenth century. As Stewart Baker, the former assistant secretary for policy at the Department of Homeland Security, argues: "I have no sympathy for privacy crusaders' ferocious objection to any new government use of technology and data." He continues: "[W]e can no longer afford the forced inefficiency of denying modern information technology to government." He then charges that privacy advocates are Luddites who "sound alarm after alarm" with the slogan "Change is bad."[7]

The *Titanic* Phenomenon

If we are mindful of the *Titanic* Phenomenon, we should think about the consequences of what can go wrong before embracing a new technology. There's a common saying that "the bigger they are, the harder they fall." Biometric data is taking identification to a whole new level, and I'm not sure we're ready for it. In addition to the concerns privacy advocates raise about government power, there's another danger to biometric identification—the possibility of a data leak or breach.

Biometrics depends upon matching people's physical characteristics to information in a database about those characteristics. Suppose you go to open a door with a fingerprint reader. You put your fingerprint on the reader, and the door opens if you're authorized to enter. The technology works by reading your fingerprint and matching it with data stored about your fingerprint in a database.[8]

If the database with your information falls into the wrong hands, then fraudsters might have your fingerprint . . . or your eye pattern or DNA. They can then use this information to spoof your identity. For example, a fraudster can fool an eye scanner by holding up a high resolution photo of a person's iris. One technologist used fingerprints left on glass to create a fake finger, which worked on the eleven fingerprint readers he tried. A study in Germany concluded that "[a]ll tested fingerprint readers were defeated with artificial fingerprints."[9] Older identification technologies, such as passwords and ID cards, can readily be changed and replaced if lost. Biometrics cannot.

The consequences of such a data leak are catastrophic because people can't readily change their fingerprints or eyes—unless they live in the science fiction world of *Minority Report.* Set in the future, the movie starred Tom Cruise as John Anderton, who lives in a society where everybody is identified by eye scans. As a person walks down the street, iris scanners detect who he is and trigger the broadcast of advertisements tailored to the passerby's profile. When a crime-prevention system predicts that Anderton will commit murder in the future, he goes on the run. To avoid detection, he gets an eye transplant.[10] In today's world, however, you can't replace your eyes. If someone obtains the data to spoof your eyes (or any other physical characteristic to identify you), you're out of luck.

To make the problem worse, the current state of data security technology is fairly poor. Since 2005 millions of records of personal information in databases have been hacked or leaked. Despite extensive media attention to the issue, the problem persists. According to one tally, 357 million records were compromised between 2005 and 2010.[11] There clearly is a problem with data security, and it shows little sign of being solved.

Biometric identification isn't inherently bad. The problem is that we don't have the appropriate legal architecture in place to use it responsibly. This isn't a Luddite argument. Instead, it's an argument that we should be better prepared to handle the new technologies we create. Those who rush headlong into embracing new security technologies strike me as being impatient. They bully anybody who calls for caution with the charge of Luddism.

I'm willing to bet that there will be some big leaks of biometric information in the future. I can see the data security breach notification letters already:

Dear John Doe:

We regret to inform you that your biometric data, including eye scan, fingerprint, DNA, and other information, has been leaked. An employee took it home on a laptop, and that computer was stolen by identity thieves. Your biometric information might be used fraudulently in the future. Please be assured we're working diligently to locate your lost data. Also be assured that we have hired scientists to develop new surgical techniques to change your eyes, fingerprints, and DNA, and that when such procedures become available, we will offer them to you at a discounted price. We sincerely apologize for the inconvenience.

Cheers,

Your Friends at the FBI

There currently isn't a good regulatory system in place to guard against abuses in the system or to provide oversight. As I've illustrated throughout this book, the law dealing with privacy and security hasn't dealt well with technologies that have already been implemented. As the technologies become more powerful, we need to improve the legal environment so that new technologies don't compound existing problems. Instead of dismissing the complaints of privacy advocates as the cries of Luddites, we should get to work on building the appropriate legal infrastructure before we implement potent new technologies.

I am not against biometric identification. The technology is more accurate than our current methods of identification. But we're not ready for biometric identification unless we have a plan in case it fails. Heeding the *Titanic* Phenomenon is a call not for stopping new technologies but for caution and thoughtfulness as we move forward.

The Fix-a-Problem Strategy

Proponents of new technologies such as biometric identification contend that we shouldn't wait to deploy these technologies because terrorism is too grave a risk. There's a real security problem, they argue, and we must act quickly to fix it.

One of the strategies behind certain arguments in favor of heightened security is to point to a problem and argue it should be fixed—what I call the "fix-a-problem strategy." Those supporting improved identification are indeed correct that our current system of identification is flawed. There is definitely a problem. Moreover, the identification problem affects security. So it is hard to counter the argument that we must improve our identification system in order to enhance security—especially when new technologies such as biometrics exist that might do so.

But there is often an unjustified assumption in the fix-a-problem strategy—that we should rush to fix the problem government officials complain about before fixing other problems. Why should the identification problem be given such a high priority? Security officials haven't explained why the identification problem is one of the

most pressing ones for security from terrorism. Improved identification might address security problems such as fraud. But it isn't clear that
faulty identification significantly facilitates terrorism. Since we don't
have infinite money and unlimited resources, we must address the
most important problems first. Unless proponents provide a convinc-
ing case for the immediate necessity of improved identification, we
should wait a little while until we're ready to handle the consequences.

Of course, we shouldn't ignore the problem. But why the
rush? We should prioritize the problems we want to fix before hurry-
ing to resolve the first one we can identify. Being careful is especially
important when the fix involves powerful new technologies that can
wreak havoc if not properly implemented.

The Case for Caution

Time and again, when new security technologies emerge, policymakers rush headfirst toward adopting them, resolving to protect privacy
but ultimately setting the issue aside to be dealt with later. The attitude seems to be to play with the technology first, then worry about its
consequences later.

Instead, I propose a different way to go about the process. We
should prepare for new technologies as diligent parents prepare for a
baby. They have the crib already set up *before* the baby arrives. Like
these diligent parents, we should be prepared before new technology
is implemented. The technologies are often not the problem—it's our
law that's the weak link. So before we rush into a debate over whether
to adopt new technologies, we should at least agree to prepare for
them first and to have a plan ready in the event they fail.

21

Conclusion

urrently, when privacy is balanced against security, the scale is rigged so that security will win out nearly every time. When we are balancing rights and liberties against government interests, it is imperative that the balancing be done appropriately. Security and privacy often clash, but there need not be a zero-sum tradeoff. There is a way to reconcile privacy and security: by placing security programs under oversight, limiting future uses of personal data, and ensuring that the programs are carried out in a balanced and controlled manner.

With awareness of the faulty arguments in the debate, with knowledge about how the law works, and with pragmatic ideas and solutions, it is possible to have a productive discussion about how to balance privacy against security. Whether you agree with me or not about how to balance privacy and security, I hope you agree that we should move past some of the stale, unproductive arguments often made in the debate. Instead of the usual arguments—the nothing-to-hide argument, the all-or-nothing fallacy, the pendulum argument—let's focus on the more meaty and important issues: What are the problems certain security measures cause for privacy and civil liberties? How can these problems be ameliorated? What kind of oversight should we have over the security measure? How effective will the security measure be? Can we protect privacy in ways that won't substantially reduce the effectiveness of the security measure?

Polltakers are asking the wrong questions, making it sound as though we must either surrender to unlimited government information gathering or let the terrorists roam free without trying to detect them. The law often is unhelpful, for it is stuck in a similar mire. The Fourth Amendment fails to protect a vast array of government information-gathering activities, and the amendment is becoming ever less relevant in the digital age. The electronic surveillance statutes are virtually obsolete. The result is that government information gathering is creating a host of problems that the law refuses to address. Regulation and oversight shouldn't turn on the happenstance of where such records are located. Changing technology that increasingly locates information outside people's homes shouldn't cause it to fall out of the regulatory regime. Instead, the law should look to the nature of the information and provide protection whenever the government's gathering of it invades privacy, inhibits First Amendment–protected activities, or causes other problems of reasonable significance.

When you cut past the rhetoric and look at the consequences, the gist of many security arguments is simply: "Don't regulate us!" When you hear critiques of the broader coverage of the Fourth Amendment or electronic surveillance statutes, focus on the consequences. The result of the triumph of such arguments will often be no oversight, no regulation, no limitation, and no accountability.

As a pragmatist, I believe that we should cut through all the game playing. When we examine a security measure, we should ask basic questions:

1. Does it work well?
2. Does it cause any problems for privacy and civil liberties?
3. What kind of oversight and regulation will resolve or ameliorate these problems?

4. If there must be a tradeoff between privacy and security, to what extent should a security measure be limited to protect privacy? How much will these limits impede the effectiveness of the security measure? Are the benefits of the regulation worth the cost in reduced effectiveness?

We must be rigorous in the way we evaluate security measures. The result might not only be better privacy protection but also more thoughtful and effective security. Curtailing ineffective security measures is often a victory not just for privacy but for security as well, since it might lead to the pursuit of better alternatives.

Some argue that we should be more trusting of our government. Despite some overreaching—even despite J. Edgar Hoover— the U.S. government never came close to becoming Big Brother. Those who would privilege security over privacy argue that fears of our descent into a totalitarian society are overblown. They contend that we should give security officials wide flexibility and discretion to respond quickly to address security threats.

But in a healthy democracy, government should never say "trust us." A healthy democratic society is one whose government never demands your blind trust. That's because strong rules and procedures are in place to ensure that the government doesn't get out of line.

There are real solutions out there, and approaches worth debating and discussing. Once we get rid of all the impediments to meaningful debate, we can finally have the kind of discussions we need to have. We can make progress in this debate when we recognize that both privacy and security are important and worth protecting.

This book isn't meant to be the end of the debate. I certainly haven't resolved all the questions. What I hope I've accomplished is to point out some of the flawed arguments in the debate and to correct myths about the law. I hope I've demonstrated how the law often forgets about the problems it must solve and the core principles it must promote.

So let the debate begin anew, but let it be more productive this time. Let's finally make some headway. If we get rid of all the noise and confusion, we can focus on what works and what doesn't. We can come to meaningful compromises. We can protect privacy as well as have effective security.

Notes

1. Introduction

1. Samuel Dash, The Intruders: Unreasonable Searches and Seizures from King John to John Ashcroft 9 (2004).

2. The maxim that the home is one's castle appeared as early as 1499. Note, *The Right to Privacy in Nineteenth Century America*, 94 Harv. L. Rev. 1892, 1894 n.18 (1981). In *Semayne's Case*, 77 Eng. Rep. 194 (K.B. 1604), the famous declaration appears that "the house of every one is to him as his castle and fortress." *Id.* at 195.

3. 4 William Blackstone, Commentaries on the Laws of England 168 (1769).

4. William J. Cuddihy, The Fourth Amendment: Origins and Original Meaning, 602–1791, at lxi (2009).

5. Tracey Maclin, *When the Cure for the Fourth Amendment Is Worse than the Disease*, 68 S. Cal. L. Rev. 1, 8 (1994); *see also* Leonard W. Levy, Origins of the Bill of Rights 158 (1999).

6. 3 The Debates in Several Conventions on the Adoption of the Federal Constitution 448–49 (Jonathan Elliot ed., 1974).

7. *See* David R. Johnson, Policing the Urban Underworld: The Impact of Crime on the Development of the American Police, 1800–1887 (1979); Eric Monkkonen, Police in Urban America, 1860–1920 (1981).

8. William J. Stuntz, *The Substantive Origins of Criminal Procedure*, 105 Yale L.J. 393, 435 (1995).

9. Curt Gentry, J. Edgar Hoover: The Man and the Secrets 111 (1991).

10. *Id.* at 112–13 (quoting Rep. J. Swagar Sherley, D-Ky.).

11. *Id.* at 113.

12. Ronald Kessler, The Bureau: The Secret History of the FBI 57 (2002).

13. The current size of the FBI can be found at the FBI's website, http://www.fbi.gov/facts_and_figures/working.htm (last visited June 6, 2010).

14. Olmstead v. United States, 277 U.S. 438, 469, 464 (1928).

15. Id. at 473, 478 (Brandeis, J. dissenting).

16. The law was section 605 of the federal Communications Act. See Communications Act of 1934, ch. 652, 48 Stat. 1064 (current version at 47 U.S.C. § 605 (2006)).

17. See Wayne R. LaFave et al., Criminal Procedure 260 (3d ed. 2000).

18. See Whitfield Diffie & Susan Landau, Privacy on the Line: The Politics of Wiretapping and Encryption 155–65 (1998).

19. Kessler, The Bureau, supra, at 166, 188.   ·

20. Gentry, Hoover, supra, at 630.

21. See 2 Hearings before the Select Committee to Study Governmental Operations with Respect to Intelligence Activities of the U.S. Senate, 94th Cong., at 10 (1976) [hereinafter Church Committee Report].

22. David Cole & James X. Dempsey, Terrorism and the Constitution 6–7 (1999).

23. Gentry, Hoover, supra, at 140–42, 126.

24. Mapp v. Ohio, 367 U.S. 643, 655 (1961).

25. United States v. Katz, 389 U.S. 347, 358 (1967).

26. Title III of the Omnibus Crime Control and Safe Streets Act of 1968, Pub. L. 90–351, § 802, 82 Stat. 197.

27. See United States v. U.S. District Court, 407 U.S. 297 (1972). This case is often referred to as the Keith case, for Judge Damon J. Keith, the federal district judge who originally heard the matter.

28. Diffie & Landau, Privacy on the Line, supra, at 178.

29. 2 Church Committee Report, supra, at 5.

30. Id. at 9–10.

31. Foreign Intelligence Surveillance Act of 1978, Pub. L. No. 95-511, § 101, 92 Stat. 1783.

32. S. Rep. No. 95-604, at 7 (1977), reprinted in 1978 U.S.C.C.A.N. 3904, 3916.

33. Office of the Attorney Gen., U.S. Dep't of Justice, Domestic Security Investigation Guidelines (1976).

34. Smith v. Maryland, 442 U.S. 735 (1979) (no reasonable expectation of privacy in a list of numbers a person dials on the phone); United States v. Miller, 425 U.S. 435, 443 (1976) (no expectation of privacy in bank records); Florida v. Riley, 488 U.S. 445 (1989) (no reasonable expectation of privacy in a greenhouse when the police flew over it in a helicopter); California v. Greenwood, 486 U.S. 35 (1988) (no reasonable expectation of privacy in abandoned trash).

35. Electronic Communications Privacy Act of 1986, Pub. L. No. 99-508, 100 Stat. 1848.

36. Uniting and Strengthening America by Providing Appropriate Tools Required to Intercept and Obstruct Terrorism (USA PATRIOT) Act of 2001, Pub. L. No. 107-56, 115 Stat. 272.

2. The Nothing-to-Hide Argument

1. Bruce Schneier, Commentary, *The Eternal Value of Privacy*, WIRED, May 18, 2006, http://www.wired.com/news/columns/1,70886-0.html (last visited Aug. 17, 2010).

2. Geoffrey R. Stone, Commentary, *Freedom and Public Responsibility*, CHI. TRIB., May 21, 2006, at 11.

3. JEFFREY ROSEN, THE NAKED CROWD: RECLAIMING SECURITY AND FREEDOM IN AN ANXIOUS AGE 36 (2004).

4. Posting of NonCryBaby to Security Focus, http://www.securityfocus.com/comments/articles/2296/18105#18105 (Feb. 12, 2003).

5. Posting of Yoven to DanielPipes.org, http://www.danielpipes.org/comments/47675 (June 14, 2006).

6. Reach For The Stars! http://greatcarrieoakey.blogspot.com/2006/05/look-all-you-want-ive-got-nothing-to.html (May 14, 2006).

7. Posting of annegb to Concurring Opinions, http://www.concurring opinions.com/archives/2006/05/is_there_a_ good.html (May 23, 2006).

8. Joe Schneider, Letter to the Editor, *NSA Wiretaps Necessary*, ST. PAUL PIONEER PRESS, Aug. 24, 2006, at 11B.

9. *NPR Day to Day: Polls Suggest Americans Approve NSA Monitoring* (NPR radio broadcast, May 19, 2006).

10. HENRY JAMES, THE REVERBERATOR (1888), *reprinted in* NOVELS, 1886–1890, at 555, 687 (1989).

11. Daniel J. Solove, *Is There a Good Response to the "Nothing to Hide" Argument?* Concurring Opinions, http://www.concurringopinions.com/ar-chives/2006/05/is_there_a_good.html (May 23, 2006).

12. *See* Comments to Daniel J. Solove, *Is There a Good Response to the "Nothing to Hide" Argument?* Concurring Opinions, http://www.concurring opinions.com/archives/2006/05/is_there_a_good.html (May 23, 2006).

13. ALEKSANDR SOLZHENITSYN, CANCER WARD 192 (Nicholas Bethell & David Burg trans., 1991).

14. FRIEDRICH DÜRRENMATT, TRAPS 23 (Richard & Clara Winston trans., 1960).

15. Posting of Andrew to Concurring Opinions, http://www.concurring opinions.com/archives/2006/05/is_there_a_good.html (Oct. 16, 2006).

16. David H. Flaherty, *Visions of Privacy: Past, Present, and Future, in*

Visions of Privacy: Policy Choices for the Digital Age 19, 31 (Colin J. Bennett & Rebecca Grant eds., 1999).

17. John Dewey, Logic: The Theory of Inquiry (1938), *in* 12 The Later Works: 1938, at 112 (Jo Ann Boydston ed., 1991).

18. I discuss the various privacy problems in more depth in my book *Understanding Privacy*, where I set forth a taxonomy to help identify the many different kinds of distinct yet related privacy problems. *See* Daniel J. Solove, Understanding Privacy (2008).

19. *See* George Orwell, Nineteen Eighty-Four (1949).

20. Franz Kafka, The Trial 50–58 (Willa & Edwin Muir trans., 1956) (1937).

21. Daniel J. Solove, The Digital Person: Technology and Privacy in the Information Age 27–75 (2004).

22. Schneier, *Eternal Value, supra*.

23. Ann Bartow, *A Feeling of Unease about Privacy Law*, 155 U. Pa. L. Rev. PENNumbra 52, 62 (2006), http://www.pennumbra.com/responses/11-2006/Bartow.pdf.

3. The All-or-Nothing Fallacy

1. *Wartime Executive Power and the National Security Agency's Surveillance Authority: Hearing before the S. Comm. on the Judiciary*, 109th Cong. 15 (2006) (statement of Alberto Gonzales, U.S. Attorney General).

2. Eric A. Posner & Adrian Vermeule, Terror in the Balance: Security, Liberty, and the Courts 12 (2007).

3. Bob Sullivan, *Have You Been Wiretapped?* MSNBC.com, Jan. 10, 2006, http://redtape.msnbc.com/2006/01/have_you_been_w.html (last visited Aug. 17, 2010) (quotation marks omitted).

4. *National Security Agency*, Rasmussen Reports, Dec. 28, 2005, http://www.rasmussenreports.com/2005/NSA.htm (last visited Aug. 17, 2010).

4. The Danger of Deference

1. MacWade v. Kelly, 460 F.3d 260, 273, 274 (2d Cir. 2006).

2. Timothy Williams & Sewell Chan, *In New Security Move, New York Police to Search Commuters' Bags*, N.Y. Times, July 21, 2005, at A1.

3. Richard A. Posner, Not a Suicide Pact: The Constitution in a Time of National Emergency 37 (2006).

4. Eric A. Posner & Adrian Vermeule, Terror in the Balance: Security, Liberty, and the Courts 5 (2007).

5. *See id.* at 6, 31, 18.

6. John Mueller, Overblown: How Politicians and the Terrorism

INDUSTRY INFLATE NATIONAL SECURITY THREATS, AND WHY WE BELIEVE THEM 13 (2006).

7. *See* BRUCE SCHNEIER, BEYOND FEAR: THINKING SENSIBLY ABOUT SECURITY IN AN UNCERTAIN WORLD 239 (2003).

8. See, for example, Arialdi M. Miniño, Melonie P. Heron & Betty L. Smith, *Deaths: Preliminary Data for 2004*, NAT'L VITAL STATS. REP., June 28, 2006, at 1, 30 tbl. 7 (2006), *available at* http://www.cdc.gov/nchs/data/nvsr/nvsr54/ nvsr54_19.pdf.

9. *See* Jeordan Legon, *Survey: "Shark Summer" Bred Fear, Not Facts*, CNN.com, Mar. 14, 2003, http://www.cnn.com/2003/TECH/science/03/13/shark. study/ (last visited Aug. 17, 2010).

10. Bruce Schneier, *Beyond Security Theater*, Schneier on Security, Nov. 13, 2009, http://www.schneier.com/blog/archives/2009/11/beyond_security.html (last visited Aug. 17, 2010).

5. Why Privacy Isn't Merely an Individual Right

1. Smith v. City of Artesia, 772 P.2d 373, 376 (N.M. Ct. App. 1989).

2. THOMAS I. EMERSON, THE SYSTEM OF FREEDOM OF EXPRESSION 545, 549 (1970).

3. Charles Fried, *Privacy*, 77 YALE L.J. 475, 478 (1968); *see also* BEATE RÖSSLER, THE VALUE OF PRIVACY 117 (R. D. V. Glasgow trans., 2005) ("Respect for a person's privacy is respect for her as an autonomous subject."); Stanley I. Benn, *Privacy, Freedom, and Respect for Persons, in* NOMOS XIII: PRIVACY 1, 26 (J. Roland Pennock & John W. Chapman eds., 1971) ("[R]espect for someone as a person, as a chooser, implie[s] respect for him as one engaged on a kind of self-creative enterprise, which could be disrupted, distorted, or frustrated even by so limited an intrusion as watching.").

4. *See, e.g.*, Rakas v. Illinois, 439 U.S. 128 (1978) (police search of car's glove compartment turns up evidence against car's passenger but passenger lacks standing to challenge the search).

5. AMITAI ETZIONI, THE LIMITS OF PRIVACY 196, 187–88, 38 (1999).

6. *Id.* at 198.

7. JOHN DEWEY, ETHICS (1908), *in* 5 THE MIDDLE WORKS: 1899–1924, at 268 (Jo Ann Boydston ed., 1978).

8. JOHN DEWEY, LIBERALISM AND CIVIL LIBERTIES (1936), *in* 11 THE LATER WORKS: 1935–1937, at 373, 375 (Jo Ann Boydston ed., 1987).

9. Robert C. Post, *The Social Foundations of Privacy: Community and Self in the Common Law Tort*, 77 CAL. L. REV. 957, 968 (1989).

10. Spiros Simitis, *Reviewing Privacy in an Information Society*, 135 U. PA. L. REV. 707, 709 (1987) ("[P]rivacy considerations no longer arise out of particular individual problems; rather, they express conflicts affecting everyone."); *see also*

Julie E. Cohen, *Examined Lives: Informational Privacy and the Subject as Object*, 52 STAN. L. REV. 1373, 1427–28 (2000) ("Informational privacy, in short, is a constitutive element of a civil society in the broadest sense of that term."); Paul M. Schwartz, *Privacy and Democracy in Cyberspace*, 52 VAND. L. REV. 1609, 1613 (1999) ("[I]nformation privacy is best conceived of as a constitutive element of civil society.").

6. The Pendulum Argument

1. RICHARD A. POSNER, LAW, PRAGMATISM, AND DEMOCRACY 298 (2003).

2. Terminiello v. Chicago, 337 U.S. 1, 36 (1949) (Jackson, J. dissenting).

3. POSNER, PRAGMATISM, *supra*, at 296.

4. WILLIAM H. REHNQUIST, ALL THE LAWS BUT ONE 224 (1998).

5. AMITAI ETZIONI, THE LIMITS OF PRIVACY 25 (1999).

6. ABC News/Washington Post Poll, September 11, 2001, *reported in* AMITAI ETZIONI, HOW PATRIOTIC IS THE PATRIOT ACT? FREEDOM VERSUS SECURITY IN THE AGE OF TERRORISM 18 (2004).

7. Gallup Poll, Jan. 28–March 22, 2002, *reported in* ETZIONI, PATRIOT ACT, *supra*, at 18.

8. Floyd Abrams, *The First Amendment and the War against Terrorism*, 5 U. PA. J. CONST. L. 1, 5–6 (2002).

9. HERMAN MELVILLE, BILLY BUDD, SAILOR (AN INSIDE NARRATIVE) (Harrison Hayford & Merton M. Sealts, Jr., eds., 1962). The manuscript was unfinished at Melville's death in 1891 and was finally published in 1924.

10. Daniel Kornstein has persuasively pointed out the similarities between the drumhead court used to try Billy Budd and the secret military tribunals of the Bush administration. *See* Daniel J. Kornstein, *Life Imitates Art on Secret Tribunals*, N.Y.L.J., Nov. 28, 2001, Perspectives, at 2.

11. *See* RICHARD H. WEISBERG, THE FAILURE OF THE WORD 133–76 (1984).

12. ERIC K. YAMAMOTO ET AL., RACE, RIGHTS, AND REPARATIONS: LAW AND THE JAPANESE AMERICAN INTERNMENT 38 (2001); *see also* Eugene V. Rostow, *The Japanese American Cases—A Disaster*, 54 YALE L.J. 489 (1945).

13. Schenck v. United States, 249 U.S. 47, 52 (1919).

14. Korematsu v. United States, 323 U.S. 214, 216 (1944).

15. Hirabayashi v. United States, 320 U.S. 81, 95 (1943).

16. *See* COMMISSION ON WARTIME RELOCATION AND INTERNMENT OF CIVILIANS, PERSONAL JUSTICE DENIED (1982). The formal apology was made in Pub. L. No. 100-383, § 2(a), 102 Stat. 903 (1988).

17. *See* ELLEN SCHRECKER, MANY ARE THE CRIMES: McCARTHYISM IN AMERICA 359–415 (1998); *see also* TED MORGAN, REDS: McCARTHYISM IN TWENTIETH-CENTURY AMERICA 546–47 (2003).

18. *See, e.g.,* Sheryl Gay Stolberg, *Transcripts Detail Secret Questioning in 50's by McCarthy,* N.Y. TIMES, May 6, 2003, at A1.

19. David Cole, *Enemy Aliens,* 54 STAN. L. REV. 953, 960–61 (2002).

20. Stephen Graham, *U.S. Frees 80 Afghan Detainees,* PHILA. INQUIRER, Jan. 17, 2005, at A12.

21. Hamdi v. Rumsfeld, 524 U.S. 507, 535 (2004).

22. *See, e.g.,* Eric Lichtblau, *U.S. Report Faults the Roundup of Illegal Immigrants after 9/11,* N.Y. TIMES, June 3, 2003, at A1.

23. Jerry Markon, *U.S. to Free Hamdi, Send Him Home,* WASH. POST, Sept. 23, 2004, at A1.

24. POSNER, PRAGMATISM, *supra,* at 304.

25. *See* ELLEN SCHRECKER, THE AGE OF MCCARTHYISM: A BRIEF HISTORY WITH DOCUMENTS 76–86 (1994); *see also* Seth F. Kreimer, *Sunlight, Secrets, and Scarlet Letters: The Tension between Privacy and Disclosure in Constitutional Law,* 140 U. PA. L. REV. 1, 13–71 (1991).

7. The National-Security Argument

1. *Continued Oversight of the USA PATRIOT Act: Hearing before the S. Comm. on the Judiciary,* 109th Cong. (2005) (testimony of Anthony C. McCarthy, Att'y, Foundation for the Defense of Democracies), *available at* http://judiciary.senate.gov/hearings/testimony.cfm?id=1493&wit_id=4260 (last visited Aug. 19, 2010); *see also* ERIC A. POSNER & ADRIAN VERMEULE, TERROR IN THE BALANCE: SECURITY, LIBERTY, AND THE COURTS 18 (2006) (arguing that when national security is at issue, there "is a premium on the executive's capacities for swift, vigorous, and secretive action").

2. Trevor W. Morrison, *The Story of United States v. U.S. District Court (Keith): The Surveillance Power, in* PRESIDENTIAL POWER STORIES 287, 292 (Christopher Schroeder & Curtis Bradley eds., 2008).

3. U.S. CONST. art II. § 1.

4. United States v. U.S. District Court (Keith), 407 U.S. 297, 320 (1972).

5. *Id.* at 322, 323.

6. Stephen I. Vladeck, *National Security's Distortion Effects,* 32 W. NEW ENG. L. REV. 285, 288 (2010).

7. Kirk Semple, *Padilla Gets 17 Years in Conspiracy Case,* N.Y. TIMES, Jan. 23, 2008, at A14.

8. Michael Brick, *Man Crashes Plane into Texas IRS Office,* N.Y. TIMES, Feb. 18, 2010, at A14.

9. United States v. Ehrlichman, 546 F.2d 910, 926 (D.C. Cir. 1976).

10. *See* New York Times Co. v. United States, 403 U.S. 713 (1971); *see also* A CULTURE OF SECRECY: THE GOVERNMENT VERSUS THE PEOPLE'S RIGHT TO

KNOW (Athan G. Theoharis ed., 1998). Attorney General John Mitchell wrote to the *New York Times* to claim that the Pentagon Papers "'will cause irreparable injury to the defense interests of the United States.'" STEPHEN DYCUS ET AL., NATIONAL SECURITY LAW 1017 (3d ed. 2002) (quoting then–Attorney General John Mitchell).

11. Brief of United States, New York Times Co. v. United States, *quoted in* LOUIS FISHER, IN THE NAME OF NATIONAL SECURITY: UNCHECKED PRESIDENTIAL POWER AND THE REYNOLDS CASE 154–55 (2006).

12. *Id. at* 156 (quoting Erwin N. Griswold, *Secrets Not Worth Keeping*, WASH. POST. Feb 15, 1989, at A25).

13. *See* United States v. Reynolds, 345 U.S. 1, 10 (1953) (holding that the government may prevent the disclosure of information if "there is a reasonable danger" that the disclosure "will expose military matters which, in the interest of national security, should not be divulged"). For more on the state secrets privilege, see Amanda Frost, *The State Secrets Privilege and Separation of Powers*, 75 FORDHAM L. REV. 1931 (2007).

14. Eric Lichtblau, *U.S. Cites "Secrets" Privilege as It Tries to Stop Suit on Banking Records*, N.Y. TIMES, Aug. 31, 2007, at A17.

15. The facts of the case are taken from El-Masri v. United States, 479 F.3d 296, 300 (4th Cir. 2007); Dana Priest, *The Wronged Man: Unjustly Imprisoned and Mistreated, Khaled al-Masri Wants Answers the U.S. Government Doesn't Want to Give*, WASH. POST, Nov. 29, 2006, at C1; Dana Priest, *Wrongful Imprisonment: Anatomy of a CIA Mistake: German Citizen Released after Months in "Rendition,"* WASH. POST, Dec. 4, 2005, at A1.

16. El-Masri v. United States, 479 F.3d 296, 309–10 (4th Cir. 2007).

17. *Id.* at 308–9, 311. The national-security law expert Robert Chesney proposes that cases involving state secrets could be heard in a "classified judicial forum." Robert M. Chesney, *State Secrets and the Limits of National Security Litigation*, 75 GEO. WASH. L. REV. 1249, 1313 (2007).

18. *Reynolds*, 345 U.S. at 10–11.

19. LOUIS FISHER, IN THE NAME OF NATIONAL SECURITY: UNCHECKED PRESIDENTIAL POWER AND THE REYNOLDS CASE xi, 28 (2006).

20. For thoughtful scholarship about government secrecy and national security, see Nathan Alexander Sales, *Secrecy and National Security Investigations*, 58 ALA. L. REV. 811 (2007); Heidi Kitrosser, *"Macro-Transparency" as Structural Directive: A Look at the NSA Surveillance Controversy*, 91 MINN. L. REV. 1163 (2007); Mary-Rose Papandrea, *Under Attack: The Public's Right to Know and the War on Terror*, 25 B.C. THIRD WORLD L.J. 35 (2005).

8. The Problem with Dissolving the Crime-Espionage Distinction

1. United States v. U.S. District Court (Keith) 407 U.S. 297, 321–22 (1972) ("[T]his case involves only the domestic aspects of national security. We

have not addressed and express no opinion as to, the issues which may be involved with respect to activities of foreign powers or their agents but that surveillance without a warrant might be constitutional in cases where the target was an agent of a foreign power.").

2. The Foreign Intelligence Surveillance Act of 1978, 50 U.S.C. §§ 1801 *et seq.* (2006). For more background about FISA, see Peter P. Swire, *The System of Foreign Intelligence Surveillance*, 72 GEO. WASH. L. REV. 1306 (2004).

3. 50 U.S.C. § 1805(a).

4. Regarding duration, compare ECPA, 18 U.S.C. § 2518(5) (orders can last up to 30 days) with FISA, 50 U.S.C. § 1805(d) (orders can last for up to 90 days and up to 120 days if a non-U.S. person is the target). Regarding notice, compare ECPA, 18 U.S.C. § 2518(8)(D) (requiring notice of surveillance) with FISA, 50 U.S.C. §§ 1806(c), 1825(b) (disclosure of surveillance only if a person is being prosecuted on the basis of evidence obtained from the surveillance or if "the Attorney General determines there is no national security interest in continuing to maintain the secrecy of the search"). Regarding the examination of the application and order for the surveillance, compare ECPA, 18 U.S.C. § 2518(9) (mandating that a defendant be allowed to inspect the court order and application for the electronic surveillance) with 50 U.S.C. § 1806(f) (calling for "review in camera and ex parte" of the "application, order, and such other materials relating to the surveillance").

5. United States v. Isa, 923 F.2d 1300 (8th Cir. 1991).

6. *Terror and Death at Home Are Caught in F.B.I. Tape*, N.Y. TIMES, Oct. 28, 1991, at A14.

7. *Isa*, 923 F.2d at 1304–6.

8. Paul Rosenzweig, *Civil Liberty and the Response to Terrorism*, 42 DUQ. L. REV. 663, 689 (2004).

9. JOHN YOO, WAR BY OTHER MEANS: AN INSIDER'S ACCOUNT OF THE WAR ON TERROR 72 (2006); *see also* STEWART BAKER, SKATING ON STILTS: WHY WE AREN'T STOPPING TOMORROW'S TERRORISM 39–69 (2010).

10. THE 9/11 COMMISSION REPORT 254–75 (2004).

11. USA PATRIOT Act, Pub. L. No. 107-56, § 204, 115 Stat. 272 (codified at 50 U.S.C. § 1804(a)(7)(B) (2006)).

12. *In re* Sealed Case, 310 F.3d 717, 720 (FISA Ct. 2002) (Only if the "government's sole objective [is] merely to gain evidence of past criminal conduct . . . the application should be denied.").

13. 50 U.S.C. § 1805(a).

14. William C. Banks & M. E. Bowman, *Executive Authority for National Security Surveillance*, 50 AM. U. L. REV. 1, 87 (2000).

15. Norman C. Bay, *Executive Power and the War on Terror*, 83 DENV. U. L. REV. 335, 373 (2005) (quoting HARRY S. TRUMAN, 1 MEMOIRS: YEAR OF DECISIONS 117 (1955)).

16. Mayfield v. United States, 599 F.3d 964 (9th Cir. 2010). I obtained some

of the facts about the case from other sources: Mayfield v. United States, 588 F.3d 1252 (9th Cir. 2010); Mayfield v. United States, 204 F. Supp. 2d 1023 (D. Or. 2007).

17. THE 9/11 COMMISSION REPORT 271 (2004). For the full discussion of the confusion, see *id.* at 254–75.

18. David S. Kris, *The Rise and Fall of the FISA Wall*, 17 STAN. L. & POL'Y REV. 487, 521–24 (2006).

19. William C. Banks, *The Death of FISA*, 91 MINN. L. REV. 1209, 1253 (2007).

9. The War-Powers Argument and the Rule of Law

1. James Risen & Eric Lichtblau, *Bush Lets U.S. Spy on Callers without Courts: Secret Order to Widen Domestic Monitoring*, N.Y. TIMES, Dec. 16, 2005, at A1.

2. JAMES BAMFORD, BODY OF SECRETS: ANATOMY OF THE ULTRA SECRET NATIONAL SECURITY AGENCY 5 (2001).

3. JAMES BAMFORD, THE SHADOW FACTORY: THE NSA FROM 9/11 TO THE EAVESDROPPING ON AMERICA 1 (2009).

4. Leslie Cauley, *NSA Has Massive Database of Americans' Phone Calls*, USA TODAY, May 11, 2006, at A1; Susan Page, *Lawmakers: NSA Database Incomplete*, USA TODAY, June 30, 2006, at A1.

5. Siobhan Gorman, *NSA's Domestic Spying Grows as Agency Sweeps up Data*, WALL ST. J., Mar. 10, 2008, at A1.

6. Prepared Statement of Hon. Alberto R. Gonzales, Attorney General of the United States, Feb. 6, 2006, *available at* http://www.justice.gov/archive/ag/speeches/2006/ag_speech_060206.html (last visited Aug. 17, 2010).

7. 50 U.S.C. § 1801.

8. Statement of Gonzales, *supra.*

9. U.S. DEP'T OF JUSTICE, WHITE PAPER, LEGAL AUTHORITIES SUPPORTING THE ACTIVITIES OF THE NATIONAL SECURITY AGENCY DESCRIBED BY THE PRESIDENT 2 (Jan. 19, 2006), *available at* http://www.justice.gov/opa/whitepaperonnsalegalauthorities.pdf.

10. Peter Baker, *President Acknowledges Approving Secretive Eavesdropping*, WASH. POST, Dec. 18, 2005, at A1.

11. William J. Stuntz, *Secret Service: Against Privacy and Transparency*, NEW REPUBLIC, Apr. 7, 2006, at 12, 15.

12. ACLU v. NSA, 493 F.3d 644, 673–74 (6th Cir. 2007).

13. *Id.* at 668.

14. 18 U.S.C. § 2511 (2006).

15. *See* Al-Haramain Islamic Foundation v. Bush, 507 F.3d 1190 (9th Cir. 2007); Hepting v. AT&T Corp., 439 F. Supp. 2d 974 (N.D. Cal. 2006).

16. Foreign Intelligence Surveillance Act of 1978 Amendments Act of 2008, Pub. L. No. 110-261, 92 Stat. 1783.

17. Jack Balkin, *The Party of Fear, the Party without a Spine, and the National Surveillance State,* Balkinization, Aug. 5, 2007, http://balkin.blogspot.com/2007/08/party-of-fear-party-without-spine-and.html (last visited Aug. 17, 2010).

10. The Fourth Amendment and the Secrecy Paradigm

1. Christopher Slobogin, Privacy at Risk: The New Government Surveillance and the Fourth Amendment 140–41 (2007).

2. *See* Daniel J. Solove, The Digital Person: Technology and Privacy in the Information Age 42 (2004).

3. U.S. Const. amend. IV.

4. According to Bureau of Justice Statistics, in 2004 (the most recent year for which data is available) there were nearly 1.1 million full-time state and local law-enforcement officers and about 105,000 full-time federal law-enforcement officials. U.S. Dep't of Justice, Bureau of Justice Statistics, Census of State and Local Law Enforcement Agencies, 2004, http://bjs.ojp.usdoj.gov/content/pub/pdf/csllea04.pdf; U.S. Dep't of Justice, Bureau of Justice Statistics, Census of Federal Law Enforcement Officers, 2004, http://bjs.ojp.usdoj.gov/content/pub/pdf/fleo04.pdf.

5. Brinegar v. United States, 338 U.S. 160, 175–76 (1949).

6. Mapp v. Ohio, 367 U.S. 643 (1961).

7. This was known as the "physical trespass doctrine." The Supreme Court held that the Fourth Amendment protected one's personal papers and documents. *See* Boyd v. United States, 116 U.S. 616 (1886). The Fourth Amendment also protected one's sealed postal letters. *See Ex Parte* Jackson, 96 U.S. 717 (1877). But if the government search or surveillance didn't involve any physical trespass to property, then there was no Fourth Amendment protection. *See* Goldman v. United States, 316 U.S. 129 (1942) (holding that the Fourth Amendment does not cover a recording device that does not physically intrude upon one's property).

8. *See* Samuel Dash, The Intruders: Unreasonable Searches and Seizures from King John to John Ashcroft 74 (2004).

9. Olmstead v. United States, 277 U.S. 438, 464 (1928).

10. *Id.* at 472, 473 (Brandeis, J. dissenting).

11. Katz v. United States, 389 U.S. 347 (1967).

12. The background facts are based on Harvey A. Schneider, *Katz v. United States, the Untold Story,* 40 McGeorge L. Rev. 13, 13–14 (2009); Brief for Respondent, *Katz v. United States,* 1967 WL 113606 (Sept. 22, 1967).

13. *Katz,* 389 U.S. at 351–52.

14. *Id.* at 361 (Harlan, J., concurring).

15. Carol S. Steiker, *Brandeis in Olmstead: "Our Government Is the Potent, the Omnipresent Teacher,"* 79 Miss. L.J. 149, 162 (2009).

16. Oliver v. United States, 466 U.S. 170 (1984).

17. United States v. Dunn, 480 U.S. 294 (1987).

18. California v. Greenwood 486 U.S. 35 (1988).

19. United States v. Scott, 975 F.2d 927 (1st Cir. 1992).

20. Florida v. Riley, 488 U.S. 445 (1989) (upholding a helicopter inspection of a greenhouse missing a few roof panels from a helicopter); *see also* California v. Ciraolo, 476 U.S. 207 (1986) (upholding a flyover inspection of a backyard).

21. United States v. Knotts, 460 U.S. 276, 281–82 (1983).

11. The Third Party Doctrine and Digital Dossiers

1. United States v. Miller, 425 U.S. 435, 443, 442 (1976).

2. Smith v. Maryland, 442 U.S. 735, 743 (1979).

3. *See* Guest v. Leis, 255 F.3d 325, 336 (6th Cir. 2001) (holding that people "lack a Fourth Amendment privacy interest in their [Internet service] subscriber information because they communicate[] it to the systems operators"); *see also* United States v. Kennedy, 81 F. Supp. 2d 1103, 1110 (D. Kan. 2000); United States v. Hambrick, 55 F. Supp. 2d 504, 508 (W.D. Va. 1999).

4. For further discussion about cloud computing and privacy, see Nicole A. Ozer & Chris Conley, Cloud Computing: Storm Warning for Privacy? (2010) (report for the ACLU of Northern California), *available at* http://ssrn.com/abstract=1611820.

5. *See In re* Jet Blue Airways Corp. Privacy Litigation, 379 F. Supp. 2d 299, 305 (E.D.N.Y. 2005); Dyer v. Northwest Airlines Corp., 334 F. Supp. 2d 1196, 1197, 1199 (D.N.D. 2004).

6. Protecting Your Personal Information, U.S. Census 2010, http://2010.census.gov/2010census/privacy/index.php (last visited Aug. 17, 2010).

7. *See* Daniel J. Solove, The Digital Person: Technology and Privacy in the Information Age 202–9 (2004).

8. *See* Hoffa v. United States, 385 U.S. 293 (1966) (holding that the Fourth Amendment provided no protection when an undercover informant befriended James Hoffa and gleaned information from him); Lewis v. United States, 385 U.S. 206 (1966) (holding that the Fourth Amendment provided no protection when the defendant invited an undercover agent into his home).

9. For an extensive examination of the breach-of-confidentiality tort, *see* Neil M. Richards & Daniel J. Solove, *Privacy's Other Path: Recovering the Law of Confidentiality*, 96 Geo. L.J. 123 (2007).

10. Orin S. Kerr, *The Case for the Third-Party Doctrine*, 107 Mich. L. Rev. 561, 573–77 (2009).

11. U.S. Const. amend. IV. For some excellent critiques of the third party doctrine, see Christopher Slobogin, Privacy at Risk: The New Government Surveillance and the Fourth Amendment 151–64 (2007); *see also* Richard A.

Epstein, *Privacy and the Third Hand: Lessons from the Common Law of Reasonable Expectations*, 24 Berkeley Tech. L.J. 1199 (2009); Jack I. Lerner & Deirdre K. Mulligan, *Taking the "Long View" on the Fourth Amendment: Stored Records and the Sanctity of the Home*, 2008 Stan. Tech. L. Rev. 3 (2008); Susan Freiwald, *First Principles of Communications Privacy*, 2007 Stan. Tech. L. Rev. 3; Stephen E. Henderson, *Beyond the (Current) Fourth Amendment: Protecting Third-Party Information, Third Parties, and the Rest of Us Too*, 34 Pepp. L. Rev. 975 (2007); Susan W. Brenner & Leo L. Clarke, *Fourth Amendment Protection for Shared Privacy Rights in Stored Transactional Data*, 14 J.L. & Pol'y 211 (2006).

12. The Failure of Looking for a Reasonable Expectation of Privacy

1. For a fuller statement of the facts, see State v. Athan, 158 P.3d 27 (Wash. 2007).

2. *Id.* at 374. A link to the letter appears in Tracy Johnson, *Ruse to Get Suspect's DNA Upheld—"Very Scary," Privacy Expert Says*, Seattle Post-Intelligencer, May 10, 2007, and is available at http://www.seattlepi.com/dayart/PDF/dna2.pdf.

3. California v. Greenwood, 486 U.S. 35 (1988) (holding that there is no reasonable expectation in the contents of garbage bags left on the curb because they are abandoned); *see also* Elizabeth E. Joh, *Reclaiming "Abandoned" DNA: The Fourth Amendment and Genetic Privacy*, 100 Nw. U. L. Rev. 857 (2006).

4. Commonwealth v. Ewing, 854 N.E.2d 993, 1001 (Mass. App. Ct. 2006).

5. Commonwealth v. Cabral, 866 N.E.2d 429, 432 (Mass. App. Ct. 2007).

6. Katz v. United States, 389 U.S. 347, 361 (1967) (Harlan, J., concurring).

7. *See, e.g.*, Susan W. Brenner, *The Fourth Amendment in an Era of Ubiquitous Technology*, 75 Miss. L.J. 1 (2005) (critiquing Court's conception of privacy as inadequate to deal with new technology); Brian J. Serr, *Great Expectations of Privacy: A New Model of Fourth Amendment Protection*, 73 Minn. L. Rev. 583, 642 (1989) (arguing that "the Court's current fourth amendment analysis is based on simplistic and logically incorrect theories of public exposure"); *see also* Lewis R. Katz, *In Search of a Fourth Amendment for the Twenty-First Century*, 65 Ind. L.J. 549, 554–55 (1990) ("[W]e should return to the privacy test intended by Stewart and Harlan and to the underlying values that motivated it.").

8. Sherry F. Colb, *What Is a Search? Two Conceptual Flaws in Fourth Amendment Doctrine and Some Hints of a Remedy*, 55 Stan. L. Rev. 119, 122 (2002); *see also* Gerald G. Ashdown, *The Fourth Amendment and the "Legitimate Expectation of Privacy,"* 34 Vand. L. Rev. 1289, 1321 (1981); Richard G. Wilkins, *Defining the "Reasonable Expectation of Privacy": An Emerging Tripartite Analysis*, 40 Vand. L. Rev. 1077, 1080 (1987). But see Orin S. Kerr, *Four Models of Fourth Amendment Protection*, 60 Stan. L. Rev. 503 (2007).

9. William James, Pragmatism 22, 23 (1991) (originally published in 1907).

10. *See* Olmstead v. United States, 277 U.S. 438, 464 (1928).

11. Katz v. United States, 389 U.S. 347, 361 (1967) (Harlan, J. concurring) (articulating the reasonable expectation of privacy test).

12. Christopher Slobogin & Joseph E. Schumacher, *Reasonable Expectations of Privacy and Autonomy in Fourth Amendment Cases: An Empirical Look at "Understandings Recognized and Permitted by Society,"* 42 Duke L.J. 727, 774 (1993).

13. Many authors have commented on the circularity of the reasonable expectation of privacy test. *See, e.g.*, Richard A. Posner, *The Uncertain Protection of Privacy by the Supreme Court*, 1979 Sup. Ct. Rev. 173, 188 (arguing that whether a person has a reasonable expectation of privacy is "circular" because "such an expectation will depend on what the legal rule is"); Robert C. Post, *Three Concepts of Privacy*, 89 Geo. L.J. 2087, 2094 (2001) ("[J]udicial interpretations of 'reasonable expectations' will affect the actions of law enforcement agencies, which in turn will affect the actual social norms that define privacy."); *see also* Michael Abramowicz, *Constitutional Circularity*, 49 UCLA L. Rev. 1, 60–61 (2001) ("Fourth Amendment doctrine . . . is circular, for someone can have a reasonable expectation of privacy in an area if and only if the Court has held that a search in that area would be unreasonable."); Anthony G. Amsterdam, *Perspectives on the Fourth Amendment*, 58 Minn. L. Rev. 349 (1974) (noting that the government could diminish expectations of privacy by announcing on television each night that we could all be subject to electronic surveillance).

14. Bond v. United States, 529 U.S. 334, 336, 338 (2000).

15. John Dewey, Logic: The Theory of Inquiry (1938), *in* 12 Later Works, 1925–1953, at 1, 110–13 (Jo Ann Boydston ed. 1986).

16. William J. Cuddihy, The Fourth Amendment: Origins and Original Meaning 602–1791, at 770 (2009).

17. *See, e.g.*, Michelle Hibbert, *DNA Databanks: Law Enforcement's Greatest Tool?*, 34 Wake Forest L. Rev. 767, 768 (1999) (noting that a DNA profile "not only reveal[s] extensive genetic information about the individual whose 'genetic fingerprint' is on file, but also about his or her close relatives"); Sonia M. Suter, *Disentangling Privacy from Property: Toward a Deeper Understanding of Genetic Privacy*, 72 Geo. Wash. L. Rev. 737, 774 (2004) (DNA influences our "temperament, health, capacities, and physical appearance").

13. The Suspicionless-Searches Argument

1. Bourgeois v. Peters, 387 F.3d 1303, 1311–12 (11th Cir. 2004).

2. *See* Terry v. Ohio, 392 U.S. 1, 27 (1968).

3. *See* Brinegar v. United States, 338 U.S. 160, 175–76 (1949) (probable cause exists "where the facts and circumstances within [law enforcement officials'] knowledge and of which they had reasonably trustworthy information [are] suffi-

cient in themselves to warrant a man of reasonable caution in the belief that an offense has been or is being committed").

4. Clifford D. May, *Two Americas and a War*, WASH. TIMES, Mar. 14, 2008, at A18.

5. Glenn Sulmasy & John Yoo, *Katz and the War on Terrorism*, 41 U.C. DAVIS L. REV. 1219, 1232 (2008).

6. Curtis Bradley, *Two Models of the Fourth Amendment*, 83 MICH. L. REV. 1468, 1473 (1985).

7. Treasury Employees v. Von Raab, 489 U.S. 656, 665–66 (1989).

8. *See* Delaware v. Prouse, 440 U.S. 648 (1979) (holding that fixed sobriety checkpoints without particularized suspicion are acceptable under the Fourth Amendment); *see also* Illinois v. Lidster, 540 U.S. 419 (2004) (upholding a checkpoint program to obtain information about a hit-and-run accident).

9. William J. Stuntz, *O. J. Simpson, Bill Clinton, and the Transsubstantive Fourth Amendment*, 114 HARV. L. REV. 842, 848 (2001).

10. Wilson v. Layne, 526 U.S. 603, 605 (1999).

11. Erik Luna, *The Overcriminalization Phenomenon*, 54 AM. U. L. REV. 703, 712 (2005).

12. *See* Alex Kozinski & Misha Tseytlin, *You're (Probably) a Federal Criminal*, *in* IN THE NAME OF JUSTICE 43 (Timothy Lynch ed., 2009).

13. HARVEY A. SILVERGLATE, THREE FELONIES A DAY: HOW THE FEDS TARGET THE INNOCENT (2009).

14. Luna, *Overcriminalization, supra*, at 712.

15. Most prosecution for drug crimes involve drug trafficking, but possession is also a crime that carries potential imprisonment. Fewer than four hundred people are convicted of possession each year. Kozinski & Tseytlin, *Federal Criminal, supra*, at 46–47.

16. DAVID G. MYERS, EXPLORING SOCIAL PSYCHOLOGY 15–19 (1994).

17. JAMES W. KALAT, INTRODUCTION TO PSYCHOLOGY 270 (8th ed. 2008).

18. *See* DANIEL L. SCHACTER, THE SEVEN SINS OF MEMORY: HOW THE MIND FORGETS AND REMEMBERS 146–47 (2001).

19. Stuntz, *Fourth Amendment, supra*, at 848.

20. AKHIL REED AMAR, THE CONSTITUTION AND CRIMINAL PROCEDURE 31 (1997).

21. Anthony G. Amsterdam, *Perspectives on the Fourth Amendment*, 58 MINN. L. REV. 349, 415 (1974). The legal scholar Fabio Arcila aptly observes that current Fourth Amendment protection "veers wildly between two opposing poles." It either strictly requires warrants with probable cause or reasonableness, *or* an "unconstrained balancing through a totality-of-the-circumstances approach." Fabio Arcila, Jr., *The Death of Suspicion*, 51 WM. & MARY L. REV. 1275, 1341 (2010).

22. As one scholar has argued, a "'reasonableness' standard, which Amar

would substitute for probable cause, is more amorphous still. Instead of focusing on only one factor (the strength of the government's case), a reasonableness standard asks the police to evaluate the interaction of numerous factors, including the degree of the invasion, the seriousness of the crime, and the need for the evidence. The result is that every case will necessarily be unique, and resolution of any given case will provide little guidance for how the next case should be resolved. Officers themselves may therefore be better off with a rule that requires prior approval of individual cases and discourages them from trying to generalize from past cases." Louis Michael Seidman, *Akhil Amar and the (Premature?) Demise of Criminal Procedure Liberalism*, 107 YALE L.J. 2281, 2296 (1998)

23. *See* Draper v. United States, 358 U.S. 307, 310–14 (1958).

24. The legal scholar Paul Ohm argues that the Fourth Amendment should be interpreted to provide a right to delete. He concludes: "The text of the Fourth Amendment seems broad enough to protect this 'right to destroy' or, in the computer context, 'right to delete' by its terms through its prohibition on unreasonable seizure." Paul Ohm, *The Fourth Amendment Right to Delete*, 119 HARV. L. REV. F. 10, 14 (2005). Viktor Mayer-Schönberger, a professor at the National University of Singapore's Lee Kuan Yew School of Public Policy, makes an extensive argument for the virtues of deleting data. *See* VIKTOR MAYER-SCHÖNBERGER, DELETE: THE VIRTUE OF FORGETTING IN THE DIGITAL AGE (2009).

14. Should We Keep the Exclusionary Rule?

1. *See* Arnold H. Loewy, *The Fourth Amendment as a Device for Protecting the Innocent*, 81 MICH. L. REV. 1229 (1983); Tracey Maclin, *When the Cure for the Fourth Amendment Is Worse than the Disease*, 68 S. CAL. L. REV. 1 (1994).

2. The Court originally adopted the exclusionary rule in 1914, in *Weeks v. United States*, 232 U.S. 383 (1914), but the rule applied only to the federal government.

3. Mapp v. Ohio, 367 U.S. 643 (1961).

4. The facts of the case are derived from SAMUEL DASH, THE INTRUDERS: UNREASONABLE SEARCHES AND SEIZURES FROM KING JOHN TO JOHN ASHCROFT 93–97 (2004).

5. *Mapp*, 367 U.S. at 659.

6. Yale Kamisar, *Mapp v. Ohio: The First Shot Fired in the Warren Court's Criminal Procedure "Revolution," in* CRIMINAL PROCEDURE STORIES 45, 76 (Carol S. Steiker ed., 2006).

7. People v. Defore, 150 N.E. 585, 587 (N.Y. 1926).

8. United States v. Leon, 468 U.S. 897, 907 n.6 (1984) (noting that 1–2 percent of felony arrestees are not convicted because of the exclusionary rule).

9. *See generally* L. Timothy Perrin, H. Mitchell Caldwell, Carol A. Chase, & Ronald W. Fagan, *If It's Broken, Fix It: Moving beyond the Exclusionary Rule*, 83 IOWA L. REV. 669 (1998).

10. Christopher Slobogin, *Why Liberals Should Chuck the Exclusionary Rule*, 1999 U. ILL. L. REV. 363, 368–401 (1999).

11. Guido Calabresi, *The Exclusionary Rule*, 26 HARV. J. L. & PUB. POL'Y 111, 112 (2002).

12. Kamisar, *Mapp, supra*, at 99.

13. Perrin et al., *Exclusionary Rule, supra*, at 735.

14. CRAIG M. BRADLEY, THE FAILURE OF THE CRIMINAL PROCEDURE REVOLUTION 104–12, 115, 123 (1993).

15. *Id.* at 130.

15. The First Amendment as Criminal Procedure

1. The First Amendment says that "Congress shall make no law respecting an establishment of religion, or prohibiting the free exercise thereof; or abridging the freedom of speech, or of the press; or the right of the people peaceably to assemble, and to petition the Government for a redress of grievances." U.S. CONST. amend. I.

2. *See, e.g.*, Marcus v. Search Warrant, 367 U.S. 717, 729 (1961) ("The Bill of Rights was fashioned against the background of knowledge that unrestricted power of search and seizure could also be an instrument for stifling liberty of expression.").

3. Larry D. Eldridge, *Before Zenger: Truth and Seditious Speech in Colonial America, 1607–1700*, 39 AM. J. LEGAL HIST. 337, 337 (1995).

4. For a description of the Zenger trial, see 1 RODNEY A. SMOLLA, LAW OF DEFAMATION § 1:28, at 1-24.1 to 1-26 (2d ed. 2000 & Supp. 2005).

5. William R. Glendon, *The Trial of John Peter Zenger*, 68 N.Y. ST. B.J., 48, 52 (Dec. 1996).

6. Wilkes v. Wood, (1763) 98 Eng. Rep. 489 (K.B.), 19 HOWELL'S STATE TRIALS 1153.

7. *See generally* ARTHUR H. CASH, JOHN WILKES: THE SCANDALOUS FATHER OF CIVIL LIBERTY (2006).

8. William J. Stuntz, *The Substantive Origins of Criminal Procedure*, 105 YALE L.J. 393, 398 (1995). For more information on the Wilkes case, see TELFORD TAYLOR, TWO STUDIES IN CONSTITUTIONAL INTERPRETATION 29–35 (1969).

9. Stuntz, *Substantive Origins, supra*, at 398–99.

10. *See* WILLIAM J. CUDDIHY, THE FOURTH AMENDMENT: ORIGINS AND ORIGINAL MEANING 602–1791, at 651–52 (2009).

11. *Wilkes*, 98 Eng. Rep. at 498, 19 HOWELL'S STATE TRIALS at 1167.

12. *See* CUDDIHY, FOURTH AMENDMENT, *supra*, at 927–30, 942.

13. *See* Akhil Reed Amar, *The Bill of Rights as a Constitution*, 100 YALE L.J. 1131, 1177 (1991) ("John Wilkes, and the author of the opinion, Lord Chief Justice Pratt (soon to become Lord Camden), were folk heroes in the colonies.").

14. Entick v. Carrington (1765), 95 Eng. Rep. 807 (K.B.), 19 HOWELL'S STATE TRIALS 1029.

15. *Id.*, 19 HOWELL'S STATE TRIALS at 1064.

16. Stuntz, *Substantive Origins, supra*, at 395.

17. Talley v. California, 362 U.S. 60, 64 (1960).

18. For more background about the right to receive ideas, see Neil M. Richards, *Intellectual Privacy*, 87 TEX. L. REV. 387 (2008); *see also* Marc Jonathan Blitz, *Constitutional Safeguards for Silent Experiments in Living: Libraries, the Right to Read, and a First Amendment Theory for an Unaccompanied Right to Receive Information*, 74 UMKC L. REV. 799 (2006); Julie E. Cohen, A *Right to Read Anonymously: A Closer Look at "Copyright Management" in Cyberspace*, 28 CONN. L. REV. 981 (1996).

19. *See* NAACP v. Alabama *ex rel.* Patterson, 357 U.S. 449, 462 (1958) ("Inviolability of privacy in group association may in many circumstances be indispensable to preservation of freedom of association, particularly where a group espouses dissident beliefs.").

20. *See* Fisher v. United States, 425 U.S. 391, 397 (1976) (holding that use of subpoena to obtain records from third party does not violate Fifth Amendment privilege of person under investigation); United States v. Dionisio, 410 U.S. 1, 9 (1973) (holding that subpoenas are not searches under Fourth Amendment).

21. *See* FED. R. CRIM. P. 17(a) ("The clerk must issue a blank subpoena— signed and sealed—to the party requesting it, and that party must fill in the blanks before the subpoena is served."); *see also In re* Subpoena Duces Tecum, 228 F.3d 341, 347–48 (4th Cir. 2000) (holding that the Fourth Amendment requires probable cause for warrants but not for subpoenas). A subpoena will be quashed on relevancy grounds if "there is no reasonable possibility that the category of materials the Government seeks will produce information relevant to the general subject of the grand jury's investigation." United States v. R. Enters., Inc., 498 U.S. 292, 301 (1991).

22. William J. Stuntz, *O. J. Simpson, Bill Clinton, and the Transsubstantive Fourth Amendment*, 114 HARV. L. REV. 842, 857–58 (2001).

23. As the Supreme Court observed in another case, "Once placed within . . . a container, a diary and a dishpan are equally protected by the Fourth Amendment." Robbins v. California, 453 U.S. 420, 425–26 (1981).

24. *See* Frederick Schauer, *Fear, Risk, and the First Amendment: Unraveling the "Chilling Effect,"* 58 B.U. L. REV. 685, 692–93 (1978) (finding chilling-effect doctrine independently significant only for "indirect governmental restriction[s] of protected expression").

25. Cases involving surveillance include Phila. Yearly Meeting of the Religious Soc'y of Friends v. Tate, 519 F.2d 1335, 1338–39 (3d Cir. 1975) (finding "immediately threatened injury to plaintiffs by way of a chilling of their rights to freedom of speech and associational privacy" when collected information was avail-

able to nonpolice parties and was disclosed on television); White v. Davis, 533 P.2d 222, 226–27 (Cal. 1975) ("[T]he presence in a university classroom of undercover officers taking notes to be preserved in police dossiers must inevitably inhibit the exercise of free speech both by professors and students.").

Cases involving chilling freedom of association include Bates v. City of Little Rock, 361 U.S. 516, 523–24 (1960) (holding that disclosure of NAACP membership lists "would work a significant interference with the freedom of association of their members" because of "uncontroverted" likelihood of ensuing "harassment and threats of bodily harm"); Shelton v. Tucker, 364 U.S. 479, 480 (1960) (invalidating a statute that required instructors to file an annual affidavit "listing without limitation every organization to which [they had] belonged or regularly contributed within the preceding five years" as a condition of employment in a state school or college); Sweezy v. New Hampshire, 354 U.S. 234, 250 (1957) ("Merely to summon a witness and compel him, against his will, to disclose the nature of his past expressions and associations is a measure of governmental interference in these matters.").

Cases involving chilling First Amendment rights generally include A Grand Jury Witness v. United States (*In re* Grand Jury Proceedings), 776 F.2d 1099, 1102–3 (2d Cir. 1985) (noting "well established" standard that government interests must be "compelling" and "sufficiently important to outweigh the possibility of infringement" when grand jury subpoena implicates First Amendment rights).

Although they don't involve the government directly, many cases hold that when a person uses a court order to compel the disclosure of the identity of an anonymous speaker, First Amendment rights are implicated. *See, e.g.,* Doe No. 1 v. Cahill, 884 A.2d 451, 457 (Del. 2005) (holding that, because of potential chilling effect, defamation plaintiffs must satisfy summary judgment standard to obtain anonymous defendant's identity); Dendrite Int'l, Inc. v. Doe, No. 3, 775 A.2d 756, 760–61 (N.J. Super. Ct. App. Div. 2001) (offering guidelines for balancing First Amendment right to anonymous speech against plaintiff's right to assert claims against actionable anonymous conduct).

26. *See* Dombrowski v. Pfister, 380 U.S. 479, 487 (1965) (finding First Amendment standing based on the threat of criminal prosecution because "[t]he chilling effect on the exercise of First Amendment rights may derive from the fact of the prosecution, unaffected by the prospects of its success or failure.").

27. For a statute "to be facially challenged on overbreadth grounds" there "must be a realistic danger that the statute itself will significantly compromise recognized First Amendment protections of parties not before the Court." Members of the City Council v. Taxpayers for Vincent, 466 U.S. 789, 801 (1984); *see also* Thornhill v. Alabama, 310 U.S. 88, 98 (1940) (holding that after arrest and conviction under overbroad statute, "[a]n accused . . . does not have to sustain the burden of demonstrating that the State could not constitutionally have written a different and specific statute covering his activities").

16. Will Repealing the Patriot Act Restore Our Privacy?

1. *See* Uniting and Strengthening America by Providing Appropriate Tools Required to Intercept and Obstruct Terrorism (USA PATRIOT) Act of 2001, Pub. L. No. 107-56, § 216, 115 Stat. 272, 288–90 (amending 18 U.S.C. § 3127(3) – (4) (2000)).

2. Orin S. Kerr, *Internet Surveillance Law after the USA Patriot Act: The Big Brother That Isn't*, 97 Nw. U. L. Rev. 607, 637 (2003).

3. Fahrenheit 9/11 (Dog Eat Dog Films 2004).

4. In my opinion, the most problematic part of the Patriot Act is its expansion of the Foreign Intelligence Surveillance Act, which I discussed in Chapter 6.

5. *See* Smith v. Maryland, 442 U.S. 735, 745–46 (1979).

6. *Compare* Wiretap Act, 18 U.S.C. §§ 2510–22 (2006) (the Wiretap Act), *and* 18 U.S.C. §§ 2701–11 (2006) (the Stored Communication Act), *with* 18 U.S.C. §§ 3121–27 (2006) (the Pen Register Act).

7. The protections of the Wiretap Act are spelled out in 18 U.S.C. § 2518.

8. 18 U.S.C. § 3123(a).

9. One court has even called the judicial role "ministerial in nature." United States v. Fregoso, 60 F.3d 1314, 1320 (8th Cir. 1995).

10. For a compelling critique of the envelope-content distinction, see Paul Ohm, *The Rise and Fall of Invasive ISP Surveillance*, 2009 U. Ill. L. Rev. 1417, 1453–55 (2009). But for a defense of the distinction, see Orin S. Kerr, *A User's Guide to the Stored Communications Act and a Legislator's Guide to Amending It*, 72 Geo. Wash. L. Rev. 1208, 1229 n.142 (2004).

11. I am referring to McLuhan's famous phrase "the medium is the message." Marshall McLuhan, Understanding Media: The Extensions of Man 7 (1964).

12. 18 U.S.C. § 3127(3) (*amended* 2001).

13. 18 U.S.C. § 3127(3), *amended by* USA PATRIOT Act, Pub. L. No. 107-56, § 216(c) (2001).

14. Kerr, *Patriot Act, supra*, at 638.

15. 18 U.S.C. § 3127(3).

16. USA PATRIOT Act § 215 (codified at 50 U.S.C. §1861(a)(1)).

17. USA PATRIOT Improvement and Reauthorization Act of 2005, Pub. L. No. 109-177, § 106(a), 120 Stat. 192, 196 (2006) (codified at 50 U.S.C. § 1861(a)(3)).

18. There are several NSL provisions in various federal statutes: (1) Electronic Communications Privacy Act, 18 U.S.C. § 2709 (2006) (FBI can compel communications companies to disclose customer information); (2) Right to Financial Privacy Act, 12 U.S.C. § 3414(a)(5) (2006) (FBI can compel financial institutions to disclose customer information); (3) Fair Credit Reporting Act, 15 U.S.C. § 1681u (2006) (FBI can compel credit reporting agencies to disclose records on individuals).

19. Barton Gellman, *The FBI's Secret Scrutiny: In Hunt for Terrorists, Bureau Examines Records of Ordinary Americans*, WASH. POST, Nov. 6, 2005, at A1.

20. For a comprehensive list of state library privacy statutes, see State Laws on the Confidentiality of Library Records, http://library-privacy.wikispaces. com/ (last visited Aug. 17, 2010).

17. The Law-and-Technology Problem and the Leave-It-to-the-Legislature Argument

1. Orin S. Kerr, *The Fourth Amendment and New Technologies: Constitutional Myths and the Case for Caution*, 102 MICH. L. REV. 801, 806 (2004); JEFFREY ROSEN, THE NAKED CROWD: RECLAIMING SECURITY AND FREEDOM IN AN ANXIOUS AGE 210 (2004) ("Congress is better suited than the courts to strike a reasonable balance between liberty and security.").

2. Kerr, *Case for Caution, supra*, at 807 ("Legislatures can enact comprehensive rules based on expert input and can update them frequently as technology changes.").

3. Right to Financial Privacy Act of 1978, 12 U.S.C. §§ 3401–3422 (2006); Fair Credit Reporting Act of 1970, 15 U.S.C. §§ 1681–1681t (2006). For a detailed discussion of why financial data is unprotected in many circumstances, see DANIEL J. SOLOVE, THE DIGITAL PERSON: TECHNOLOGY AND PRIVACY IN THE INFORMATION AGE 206 (2004).

4. Kerr, *Case for Caution, supra*, at 820.

5. Konop v. Hawaiian Airlines, 302 F.3d 868, 874 (9th Cir. 2002).

6. Kerr, *Case for Caution, supra*, at 807.

7. The problem with section 605 of the Communications Act of 1934 was that it permitted private citizens to wiretap but prohibited law-enforcement officials from using evidence of electronic surveillance for even the most serious of crimes. JAMES G. CARR & PATRICIA L. BELLIA, THE LAW OF ELECTRONIC SURVEILLANCE § 2.1, at 2–3 (2003). According to Senate Report 1097, section 605 "serves . . . neither the interests of privacy nor of law enforcement." S. Rep. No. 90-1097, at 2154 (1968).

8. The Wiretap Act provides for high civil penalties—minimum damages of $10,000 per violation. 18 U.S.C. § 2520(c)(2)(B).

9. Although the Stored Communications Act focuses on "electronic storage," 18 U.S.C. § 2701(a), the term is defined in the Wiretap Act, 18 U.S.C. § 2510(17).

10. *See* 18 U.S.C. § 3121(a).

11. 18 U.S.C. § 2510(17).

12. COMPUTER CRIME AND INTELLECTUAL PROPERTY SECTION, U.S. DEP'T OF JUSTICE, MANUAL ON SEARCHING AND SEIZING COMPUTERS AND OBTAINING ELECTRONIC EVIDENCE IN CRIMINAL INVESTIGATIONS § III.B (2001).

13. Some courts have interpreted "backup protection" more broadly. *See* Theofel v. Farey-Jones, 359 F.3d 1066, 1075–76 (9th Cir. 2004).

14. *See* United States v. Scarfo, 180 F. Supp. 2d 572, 581–82 (D.N.J. 2001).

15. *See* Peter P. Swire, *Katz Is Dead. Long Live Katz*, 102 MICH. L. REV. 904, 922 (2004) ("Dialogue and continued participation by both branches is likely to lead to better outcomes, for both majoritarian and counter-majoritarian reasons.").

16. In this approach I attempt to shift the defaults somewhat similarly to how Raymond Ku suggests that Fourth Amendment analysis be altered. He argues that Congress should statutorily authorize the government's use of technology for that use to be considered reasonable under the Fourth Amendment. Raymond Shih Ray Ku, *The Founder's Privacy: The Fourth Amendment and the Power of Technological Surveillance*, 86 MINN. L. REV. 1325, 1374–75 (2002).

18. Video Surveillance and the No-Privacy-in-Public Argument

1. SURVEILLANCE STUDIES NETWORK, A REPORT ON THE SURVEILLANCE SOCIETY FOR THE INFORMATION COMMISSIONER 19 (2006), *available at* http://www.ico.gov.uk/upload/documents/library/data_protection/practical_application/surveillance_society_full_report_2006.pdf; *see generally* CLIVE NORRIS & GARY ARMSTRONG, THE MAXIMUM SURVEILLANCE SOCIETY: THE RISE OF CCTV (1999); Jeffrey Rosen, *A Cautionary Tale for a New Age of Surveillance*, N.Y. TIMES, Oct. 7, 2001, § 6 (Magazine).

2. Alex Johnson, *Smile! More and More You're on Camera*, MSNBC.com, June 25, 2008, http://www.msnbc.msn.com/id/25355673/.

3. 18 U.S.C. § 2510(2) (2006) (defining an "oral communication" as one "uttered by a person exhibiting an expectation that such communication is not subject to interception under circumstances justifying such expectation").

4. *See, e.g.*, United States v. Falls, 34 F.3d 674, 680 (8th Cir. 1994); United States v. Koyomejian, 970 F.2d 536, 540 (9th Cir. 1992); United States v. Biasuci, 786 F.2d 504, 508 (2d Cir. 1986).

5. 50 U.S.C. § 1804(a)(6)–(a)(7) (2006).

6. United States v. Torres, 751 F.2d 875, 885 (7th Cir. 1984).

7. United States v. Mesa-Rincon, 911 F.2d 1433, 1437 (10th Cir. 1990).

8. GEORGE ORWELL, NINETEEN EIGHTY-FOUR 5–6 (1949).

9. California v. Ciraolo, 476 U.S. 207, 215 (1986).

10. For a thoughtful argument about privacy in public, see HELEN NISSENBAUM, PRIVACY IN CONTEXT: TECHNOLOGY, POLICY, AND THE INTEGRITY OF SOCIAL LIFE 113–26 (2010).

11. Jerry Kang, *Information Privacy in Cyberspace Transactions*, 50 STAN. L. REV. 1193, 1260 (1998).

12. Julie E. Cohen, *Examined Lives: Informational Privacy and the Subject as Object*, 52 STAN. L. REV. 1373, 1426 (2000).

13. *See* Christopher Slobogin, *Public Privacy: Camera Surveillance of Public Places and the Right to Anonymity*, 72 Miss. L.J. 213, 237–67 (2002); *see also* Paul M. Schwartz, *Privacy and Democracy in Cyberspace*, 52 Vand. L. Rev. 1609, 1656 (1999) ("[P]erfected surveillance of naked thought's digital expression short-circuits the individual's own process of decisionmaking.").

14. Peck v. United Kingdom, 2003-I Eur. Ct. H.R. 44.

15. Jennifer King et al., Ctr. for Info. Tech Research in the Interest of Soc'y, Univ. of Cal. Berkeley, Preliminary Findings of the Statistical Evaluation of the Crime-Deterrent Effects of the San Francisco Crime Camera Program 2–3 (2008).

16. Martin Gill & Angela Spriggs, Dev. & Statistics Directorate, Home Office Research, Assessing the Impact of CCTV 33 (2005).

19. Should the Government Engage in Data Mining?

1. Richard A. Posner, Not a Suicide Pact: The Constitution in a Time of National Emergency 141 (2006).

2. Eric Goldman, *Data Mining and Attention Consumption, in* Privacy and Technologies of Identity 225, 228 (Katherine Strandburg & Daniela Stan Raicu eds. 2006).

3. John M. Poindexter, *Finding the Face of Terror in Data*, N.Y. Times, Sept. 10, 2003, at A25.

4. William Safire, *You Are a Suspect*, N.Y. Times, Nov. 14, 2002, at A35.

5. *Pentagon's "Terror Information Awareness" Program Will End*, USA Today.com, Sept. 25, 2003, http://www.usatoday.com/news/washington/2003-09-25-pentagon-office_x.htm.

6. Shane Harris, *TIA Lives On*, Nat'l J., Feb. 25, 2006.

7. Tech. & Privacy Advisory Comm., U.S. Dep't of Defense, Safeguarding Privacy in the Fight against Terrorism 5 (2004).

8. U.S. Gen. Accounting Office, Data Mining: Federal Efforts Cover a Wide Range of Uses 2 (2004).

9. Richard A. Posner, *Our Domestic Intelligence Crisis*, Wash. Post, Dec. 21, 2005, at A31.

10. Posner, Not a Suicide Pact, *supra*, at 97.

11. Terry McDermott, Perfect Soldiers: The 9/11 Hijackers: Who They Were, Why They Did It (2005); Peter Finn, *A Fanatic's Quiet Path to Terror: Rage Was Born in Egypt, Nurtured in Germany, Inflicted on U.S.*, Wash. Post, Sept. 22, 2001, at A1.

12. *Profile: Timothy McVeigh*, BBC News, May 11, 2001, http://news.bbc.co.uk/2/hi/1321244.stm (last visited Aug. 17, 2010).

13. John Schwartz & Serge F. Kovaleski, *Bookish Recluse Lived Sparse Cabin Existence*, Wash. Post, Apr. 4, 1996, at A1.

14. *See* Fred H. Cate, *Government Data Mining: The Need for a Legal Framework*, 43 Harv. C.R.-C.L. L. Rev. 435, 474 (2008) ("Government data mining seems similarly likely to be fighting yesterday's battles—a problem that commercial data miners face to a far less extent, since the characteristics of desirable consumers are likely to change far less rapidly than those of terrorists.").

15. *See* Bureau of Transp. Statistics, Research & Innovative Tech. Admin., Passengers: All Carriers-All Airports, http://www.transtats.bts.gov/Data_Elements.aspx?Data=1 (last visited Aug. 17, 2010).

16. For more on the problem of false positives, see Bruce Schneier, Schneier on Security 9–12 (2008); Cate, *Government Data Mining, supra*, at 470–76. As Jeff Jonas, a leading technologist at IBM, and Jim Harper of the Cato Institute contend: "Data mining is not an effective way to discover incipient terrorism." Jeff Jonas & Jim Harper, Effective Counterterrorism and the Limited Role of Predictive Data Mining 2 (2006).

17. Robert O'Harrow, Jr., No Place to Hide 56–63 (2005) (discussing the lobbying efforts of Acxiom, a data brokerage company, to convince politicians of data mining's potential value for counterterrorism purposes).

18. *See* Tal Z. Zarsky, *"Mine Your Own Business!": Making the Case for the Implications of the Data Mining of Personal Information in the Forum of Public Opinion*, 5 Yale J.L. & Tech. 1, 27 (2003).

19. Frederick Schauer, Profiles, Probabilities, and Stereotypes 173–74 (2003).

20. Daniel J. Steinbock, *Data Matching, Data Mining, and Due Process*, 40 Ga. L. Rev. 1, 82 (2005); *cf.* Danielle Keats Citron, *Technological Due Process*, 85 Wash. U. L. Rev. 1249, 1254 (2008) ("The opacity of automated systems shields them from scrutiny. Citizens cannot see or debate these new rules. In turn, the transparency, accuracy, and political accountability of administrative rulemaking are lost.").

21. Louis D. Brandeis, Other People's Money and How the Bankers Use It 92 (1914).

22. Letter from James Madison to W. T. Barry (Aug. 4, 1822), *in* 9 The Writings of James Madison: 1819–1836, at 103, 103 (Gaillard Hunt ed., 1910). The quotation is modified to eliminate the archaic punctuation and capitalization.

20. The Luddite Argument, the *Titanic* Phenomenon, and the Fix-a-Problem Strategy

1. The REAL ID Act of 2005 was passed as Division B of the Emergency Supplemental Appropriations Act for Defense, the Global War on Terror, and Tsunami Relief, 2005, Pub. L. No. 109-13, 119 Stat. 231.

2. Laura Meckler, *ID Card for Workers Is at Center of Immigration Plan*, Wall St. J., Mar. 9, 2010, at A4.

3. Simon A. Cole, Suspect Identities: A History of Fingerprinting and Criminal Identification 32–59 (2001).

4. Michael Chertoff, Homeland Security: Assessing the First Five Years 119 (2009).

5. Amitai Etzioni, The Limits of Privacy 104 (1999).

6. *See generally* Jim Harper, Identity Crisis: How Identification Is Overused and Misunderstood (2006); Richard Sobel, *The Degradation of Political Identity under a National Identification System*, 8 B.U. J. Sci. & Tech. L. 37 (2002).

7. Stewart Baker, Skating on Stilts: Why We Aren't Stopping Tomorrow's Terrorism 309, 314, 315 (2010).

8. Bruce Schneier, *Real ID: Costs and Benefits*, Schneier on Security, Jan. 30, 2007, http://www.schneier.com/blog/archives/2007/01/realid_costs_an.html (last visited Aug. 17, 2010).

9. Drew Robb, *Authentication with a Personal Touch: Fingerprint Scanners Are Accurate Biometric Identification Tools—But They're Not Foolproof*, Government Computer News, Aug. 29, 2005, 2005 WLNR 26140142. For a further discussion of spoofing biometric identification systems, see Gang Wei & Dongge Li, *Biometrics: Applications, Challenges, and the Future, in* Privacy and Technologies of Identity 135, 142–45 (Katherine Strandburg & Daniela Stan Raicu eds. 2006); Ishwar K. Sethi, *Biometrics: Overview and Applications, in* Privacy and Technologies of Identity, *supra*, at 117, 131–32.

10. Minority Report (Twentieth Century Fox Film Corp. 2002) (directed by Steven Spielberg).

11. Mary Pilon, *Data Theft Hits 3.3 Million Borrowers*, Wall St. J., Mar. 29, 2010.

Index

Index

Index

Index

ABOUT THE AUTHOR

Daniel J. Solove is John Marshall Harlan Research Professor of Law, George Washington University Law School. An internationally known expert in privacy law, he is the author of several books, including *The Future of Reputation: Gossip, Rumor, and Privacy on the Internet* and *Understanding Privacy*. He lives in Washington, D.C., and blogs at http://concurringopinions.com.